Improving Your Child's Behavior

Madeline C. Hunter
Paul V. Carlson

CORWIN PRESS, INC.
A Sage Publications Company
Thousand Oaks, California

Other publications by the same author:

Mastery Teaching
Motivation Theory for Teachers
Retention Theory for Teachers
Discipline That Develops Self-Discipline
Teach More — Faster!
Teach for Transfer
Aide-ing in Education
Improved Instruction
Parent-Teacher Conferencing
Mastering Coaching and Supervision

Improving Your Child's Behavior
© Copyright 1977 by Madeline Hunter and Paul V. Carlson

Printed in the United States of America.
Tenth Printing 1996

Hunter, Madeline C.
    Improving your child's behavior / Madeline C. Hunter, Paul V. Carlson
        p.   cm.
    Originally published : Glendale, Calif. : Bowmar, 1971.
    ISBN 0-8039-6326-2   (pbk. : alk. paper)
    1. Child rearing. 2. Behavior modification. 3. Reinforcement (Psychology)
    I. Carlson, Paul V., 1933-   II. Title.
HO769.H92   1996
649'.64 — dc20   96-3742

Text design, lettering, and illustrations by Paul L. Taylor

For information on the complete Madeline Hunter Collection, please contact:

CORWIN PRESS, INC.
A Sage Publications Company
2455 Teller Road
Thousand Oaks, CA 91320-2218
e-mail: order@corwin.sagepub.com
Call: 805-499-9774   Fax: 805-499-0871

DEDICATION....

TO YOU

because you want to become A Better Parent,

this book is respectfully dedicated

PREFACE

The behavior of one human being affects the behavior of another. This fact has been known since the beginning of time. During the last half century psychologists have, through systematic investigations, discovered a method of insuring that what a person does results in what he desires and not in unexpected or undesirable consequences. As a result of what is known we can now systematically use the power of rewarding, punishing, or ignoring to strengthen or weaken behavior.

It is important to emphasize that in every family the influence of the members on each other is occurring every day. We can no more prevent this happening than we can choose not to breathe. Because their influence over the behavior of their children is inevitable, parents must be aware of four basic principles that direct and guide this influence in achieving results that are beneficial to each child.

The purpose of this book is to help parents acquire this knowledge. It is reassuring to know that what parents do *will* make a difference!

TABLE OF CONTENTS

CHAPTER I

HOW TO BEGIN

To be an effective parent is probably the most difficult task in the world. It is a task for which most of us have little or no training. Yet we are so anxious to be successful. We try to be objective and realistic; we try to approach our parental role with a minimum of prejudice and bias. Yet in no other enterprise are we so emotionally involved, so tempted to see what we would like to see rather than what actually exists, so vulnerable to the results of our handiwork, so highly visible to the world as a success or failure.

Even to those parents with much natural aptitude and many learned skills, parenthood presents a myriad of problems. But to those who through no fault of their own seem to be parental bumblefingers, life is a nightmare of worry until the years pass and the responsibility of the child rearing yoke lightens.

There is no doubt that bringing up children is difficult, but psychological knowledge is now available that makes the task easier and success in child rearing more probable. To pass some of this knowledge along to you is the aim of this book. The material was carefully selected. It deals with one extremely important part of the complex process that

you as a parent must go through to learn how to help your children develop sound behavior patterns.

There are practical principles to guide you. Think of these principles as tools. Like any set of tools they can be used or abused and can be effective or ineffective, depending on how well you use them.

WHICH ARE IDEAL BEHAVIORS?

In no way do the authors presume to tell you the values you should instill, the attitudes you should develop, the character traits you should encourage, or the habits that will guarantee success in life. This book will help you guide your child so that he will develop in the way best for him. Your own values and goals will determine which behaviors you wish your child to develop. And once you decide that, this book will help you *bring it off*.

Because you are the parent, it is essential that you become aware of the values you hold. Only by so doing can you identify the behaviors you are going to encourage or discourage in your child. For example, if you wish your son to be an independent thinker, you must realize that as he is learning he will make mistakes in judgment. He will need to be encouraged for the thinking that led to his decision, rather than to be discouraged by the less-than-perfect results. If you wish your daughter to be a warm and sympathetic person, remember that in the process of learning, she will sometimes misplace her sympathy. Again, she must be encouraged in the trait you hope to develop rather than be discouraged by her occasional lack of discrimination.

To help your child, you must focus on the behavior that really matters—the behavior that will make a difference a week, a month, or a year from now. You cannot afford to waste your energy on temporary behavior, annoying though it may be. Cleanliness and good grooming are important, but a particular style or length of skirt and hair simply reflect the times and will change. Don't waste an undue amount of emotion and energy trying to fight the temporary appearance standards of your youngster that are *in* with his age group. Instead, concentrate on the more permanent traits of cleanliness and grooming, even if you settle for obtaining these within some current fad.

There are so many things all of us would like changed in each child that we have to make choices in terms of what is most important to us and to each youngster. You may have to decide that your child's interest in his studies is more important than the tidiness of his desk. Or your child's wise choice of foods and the variety he eats will make more difference in his later life than the irritating crumbs on the table or the spilled milk. Direct your major effort to important traits. Do not dissipate too much energy on unimportant items of behavior that change with the passing of time. All of us would like the perfect child. Unfortunately, no one has been able to achieve that goal, so it is highly improbable that you will have everything come out exactly as you may wish, either.

SUMMARY

Decide on the values and behaviors you wish to encourage in your child. Some of these may be achieved slowly. And as the child grows through the various stages of development, formerly unachievable behaviors will become possible. Be sure that you are expecting behavior that is important for your child to learn, is appropriate for his age level, and falls within his ability to achieve.

CAN ALL BEHAVIOR BE CHANGED?

Not all of the behavior of your child can be controlled or directed by you. Children differ in their degree of inborn talent and capacity to develop in one direction or another. You can modify these inborn tendencies by encouraging or discouraging them, but you may not be able to change them completely. As a result, each child will vary in the way he responds to your efforts at change. Still, you will be amazed at how successful you can be if you really work at it.

Certain kinds of behavior can easily be changed. Other behavior may be quite resistant or even unchangeable. For example: You will not be able to decide that your child will be an engineer or a mechanic, a musician or a salesman, an actress or a housewife. You can, however, help your child become a *more successful* engineer, mechanic, musician, salesman, actress, or housewife. You cannot decide whether your child will be more deft with his hands, or with words and ideas. But you can help him *develop* the ability he possesses in using his hands or in expressing ideas.

Many of the undesirable behaviors in your child that you have accepted as *just like everyone else in our family* and which you feel cannot be changed, could actually have been unknowingly encouraged by you. It stands to reason that if you have unknowingly encouraged the development of this behavior, you can also learn how to discourage it, and thereby lessen or eliminate that behavior.

Let us look at an example you will probably recognize. Your child asks for something or permission to do something. It is a reasonable request that you would grant ordinarily, but you are tired, or grouchy, or annoyed at someone else, or things have not gone well. So you say, "No!"

This negative response is unreasonable and not typical of you, so your child will not accept it. He protests and argues. Or even worse, he whines and fusses. You are already feeling guilty about your unreasonable "no!"—and in your present state you cannot endure the sound of his fussing. So you capitulate with, "Oh, all right."

Although you certainly did not intend to, you have just encouraged your child to fuss and argue to get his way because it worked for him in this instance. The next time you say "no" and need to stick to it, don't be surprised if your child uses the same tactics that worked for him before. Now, let us look at how you might have handled the situation differently.

You might have said, "Stop fussing. Leave me alone for a few minutes and I'll reconsider."

Then your change to a "yes" would have encouraged peaceful behavior during your calm reconsideration. With such encouragement, the next time you are out of sorts and respond over-quickly, your child may not engage in preliminary argument. He may merely suggest leaving you alone for unpressured decision-making. And if he does not, you can certainly repeat your request for peace and quiet. By such tactics you encourage constructive behavior in your child and gradually eliminate the possibility of unwittingly teaching him to fuss and argue to get his way.

So if you have a chronic arguer or fusser in the family, you should no longer dismiss the behavior by saying, "Oh, he's just like So-and-So." Check first to see if you may actually be encouraging this behavior by your own actions.

LOVE IS NOT ENOUGH

You are reading this book because you love your child and because you want to be the most effective parent possible. You probably realize that along with your love you must also give him your respect. In return you should expect and receive the respect of your child. Love and respect must be mutual. The lack of mutual love and respect can lead to a demanding, self-centered, and lonely child.

Do you realize how much reassurance and love you provide for your child when you take the time and energy to set definite limits on his behavior? Much mutual respect and shared responsibility is encouraged in this way.

We cannot help but think of the child who was *grounded* in his own yard and proudly told his playmates over the fence, "My parents care how I grow up!" If your child sees you setting constructive limits on his behavior, he has evidence that you care what happens to him. Of course, he may find some of your decisions inconvenient, but as long as he has evidence that you really love him and are fair he will respect you for any reasonable standards you set.

No parent should leave child rearing completely to chance. This is hazardous for both child and parent. Remember, *as you increase your skill in child rearing and achieve a more effective and calmer discipline you will develop a deeper and more meaningful relationship with your child.* You will also become a happier parent. If you are too permissive and accept undesirable behavior in your child, you may slowly build up a subtle resentment in yourself that one day may explode. The resulting anger and punishment you are likely to inflict on your child only adds to his negative feelings and inappropriate behavior responses.

The principles you will meet in this book are a guide, not a cure-all. You will find that they are successful with most kinds of behavior. If you have genuinely become skillful in using the suggestions and approaches that we describe, but you feel that they do not seem to work with the problems your child presents, consultation with a psychologist or a psychiatrist may be helpful.

Do not be afraid to seek professional help for a severe behavior problem or a persistent discipline difficulty. Love your child enough to seek help when it is needed. If it is more comfortable, you might begin by consulting with your family doctor, your religious advisor, or some other specialist who is available to assist you and to work with your child.

NONE OF IT IS NEW

As you begin to read about changing your child's behavior, you may find it sobering to discover that these same principles also work effectively with your spouse, your mother-in-law, or your next door neighbor. *You are really discovering that what you do makes a predictable difference in how other people act.*

This has been happening all of your life, although you may not have been aware of it. Now that you are aware, you are able to develop the ability to use your actions more productively. It is the intent of the authors to help you help your children. If you become able to use your new skill in improving your child's behavior and in developing his abilities, you will have achieved the purpose of this book.

CHAPTER II
POSITIVE REINFORCEMENT

You are now ready to begin your instruction in the theory of improving your child's behavior. Really, there is nothing more practical than a good theory which, once understood, can be applied in almost every situation you encounter.

But first, because so many books have been written about raising children, we will mention some areas that we feel you need not concern yourself about at all. For example, it is said that parents must understand the causes of a behavior before the behavior can be changed. On the contrary, our experience indicates that it is actually very difficult or sometimes impossible for parents to identify the exact cause of most behaviors in their child. Even more important, we have found that identifying a cause is often not a necessary step in changing behavior.

Another school of thought contends that good common sense is all that parents need to raise a child. But the children of such parents, in our experience, are testimony that this approach is futile. The difficulty is that there is apparently nothing *less* common than good common sense. It is a mistake to believe that becoming parents somehow infuses us with the instant ability to rear children successfully.

SOMETHING WORTH TRYING

The theory that we have found most helpful to parents in improving a child's behavior is called **reinforcement theory.** Applying the four principles of this theory can make the difference between enjoying parenthood and merely enduring it, between children who are a pleasure and those who are not, between increasing your child's desirable traits and just hoping things will turn out well. Consistent and systematic use of the four principles can produce amazingly fast, effective, and permanent changes in children.

Of course, we do not say that reinforcement theory is the only answer. We have found it to be the most useful answer available to all of us at this stage of the research in child development. Complaints such as "She won't eat"—"He doesn't mind"—"They don't come home on time!"—"Her room is a mess!" are typical of the conditions that can be helped by using reinforcement *know-how.*

Are you ready to start?

LET'S GET DOWN TO CASES

The first principle for you to become acquainted with is **positive reinforcement.** Positive reinforcement is accomplished through the use of **positive reinforcers.**

A positive reinforcer can be anything that is desired or needed by the child. The child can want praise, attention, food, approval, toys, special privileges, etc. When you use it, a *positive reinforcer will strengthen the behavior it immediately follows and make that behavior more likely to happen again.* Strengthening a behavior by using a positive reinforcer is called positive reinforcement.

When Johnny, working diligently, finishes a job and his mother says, "Good for you!" finishing the job is the behavior. "Good for you!" is the positive reinforcer (because Johnny wants praise) that makes the behavior more likely to reoccur. Praising Johnny when he finishes a job will make him more apt to do it again.

In psychological terms we would explain it like this: When a positive reinforcer ("Good for you!") immediately follows behavior (finishing his job) the positive reinforcer strengthens behavior and increases the chances that the behavior will occur again (Johnny will be more likely to finish his job next time).

The positive reinforcer should follow the behavior *immediately* to be effective. Saying "Good for you!" after a lapse of time will not achieve the same effect.

LET'S CHECK STEP ONE

Because this information will not be useful unless you are able to develop it into a skill, we have carefully planned this book to help you apply each principle correctly as you go along.

We have provided you with practice situations. Each situation has several solutions. Select one answer that seems correct to you. Beside that answer will be the number of the page where you can turn to find out if you chose the best answer. Any answer you select will explain something about the situation, so do not think of the answers as being only right or wrong.

Look at problem one on this page. Select an answer, then turn to the page indicated. If you have selected the best answer, **you will be positively reinforced** by your choice and will be directed to the next page of text in the book. If your answer is not the best one, you will be told what is wrong about it and will be directed back to the situation to select a better answer.

ONE

We use a positive reinforcer because:

[a] **It will make our child more comfortable** turn to page 18, top.

[b] **The parent becomes a pleasant person** turn to page 18, bottom.

[c] **It will strengthen the behavior it follows** turn to page 19, top.

[d] **A positive approach is always the best** turn to page 19, bottom.

[1a] You chose **it will make our child more comfortable.**

It usually does, but so would giving him candy and doughnuts or leaving him alone and not expecting anything. There is a more important reason for using positive reinforcers. Go back to the statement on page 17, and select a reason you think is more important.

[1b] You chose **the parent becomes a pleasant person.**

You may become a more pleasant person, or you may blow your top in frustration because you have to act as if things are going well even when they are not. There is a more important reason for using positive reinforcers. Go back to the statement on page 17, and select the reason you think is more important.

[1c] You chose **it will strengthen the behavior it follows.**

GOOD FOR YOU! We want to strengthen your behavior of selecting the right answer. Yes, while there are all sorts of wholesome side effects, the main reason we use positive reinforcers is that we want to increase the likelihood of a certain behavior recurring. We want the child to do it again. You are ready to turn to page 20, and continue.

[1d] You chose **a positive approach is always the best.**

Usually it is, but not always. You will learn why later in this book. There is a more important reason for using positive reinforcers. Go back to page 17, and select the reason you think is more important.

NOW FOR STEP TWO

In Step One you found out what you can do to reinforce your child's desirable behavior and increase the likelihood that such behavior will happen again.

Now we come to the second step. How do you make that positively reinforced behavior *permanent?*

Step Two hinges importantly on your behavior as a parent. You must be vigilant and consistent. *When your child behaves in a way that you want, immediate positive reinforcers will increase the likelihood that he will keep on behaving in the desirable way.*

You will no doubt agree with what has just been said, if you think about it. Yet the daily behavior of parents does not always follow it. Frequently they operate on the assumption that behaving correctly is only what a child *should* be doing, so they forget to positively reinforce good behavior and just ignore it.

Let us look at an example. Suppose you take your child out visiting and he behaves well. Usually you take it for granted that this is the way it should be, and you do nothing. It is only when he misbehaves that you do something.

Ignoring desirable behavior (the absence of reinforcement) does nothing to encourage proper behavior in your child. What you should do is to positively reinforce the child's good behavior, so that he will continue to behave well when he is out with you. You should let your child know that you have noticed, and have really appreciated his proper behavior. What better way to increase the incidence of that desirable behavior! After all, a child is not so very different from you. If you receive a compliment on something you are doing (or wearing), doesn't the compliment make you want to do it again?

Let us look at another example, one that is all too typical. Your son comes to the dinner table, and you see that he is disheveled and has obviously unwashed hands. You *do something*. The next day he again comes to dinner in an unsanitary condition. You *do something* again. On the third day, when he comes to the table grimy once more, your patience has ended. You have reached your PBT (Parent Blows Top) point and you DO SOMETHING.

After that your son is convinced that you mean business. So on the fourth day he comes in washed and combed and settles down at the table properly to avoid the SOMETHING. And this is where you fall into your self-defeating trap. "Thank goodness," you think to yourself. And you proceed to enjoy your meal.

The next day your son has reverted to his old sloppy behavior. Why shouldn't he? When he acted appropriately (washed before dinner), you did absolutely nothing to increase the likelihood that he would continue to act that way. So his old habits took over. If you wish his neat behavior to happen again, you must positively reinforce it. You must say, "You look just right!" or "You're really growing up!" or whatever he would like to hear when he behaves appropriately.

But remember, positive reinforcers must be sincere. Children can always detect phony compliments. Look for the behavior you can really praise, whether it is his appearance, his effort, or merely his intention. "I know you are trying because even if you didn't get all the dirt off—you remembered you should wash your hands." This remark takes positive note of the child's effort, but very carefully avoids over-praising where the child knows it is not true.

WHAT HAVE YOU LEARNED?

Let us try a practice situation to check Steps One and Two. Read the example on the next page, select the answer that you think is best, and find out what the authors have to say about it.

TWO

All parents have had experience with a child who interrupts, thereby spoiling conversation for everyone else and putting a great strain on your disposition. You tell the child he must wait until you are through. You insist that he must wait. He finally does wait, and you figure it's about time he gets the point and remains quiet. Because he has already interrupted so many times, you don't acknowledge his good manners in waiting, but go on with what you are trying to say. You feel that his silence is only your just due. And once you have him quiet, you feel you can continue the conversation without him and give someone else a chance to speak.

During subsequent conversations, the child again interrupts. This is probably because:

[a] He has had the habit so long it will take time to get over it_____turn to page 23, top.

[b] He has never learned to wait_____turn to page 23, bottom.

[c] You did not positively reinforce the behavior you wished him to continue_____turn to page 24, top.

[d] He is angry because you did not listen to him_____turn to page 24, bottom.

[2a] You chose **he has had the habit so long it will take time to get over it.**

No doubt it will take time. But he will never get over it if, when he tries the right behavior and waits quietly, it does not turn out well for him. Suppose you tried a new recipe and it was a failure. You would not keep on using it, would you? Turn back to the situation on page 22. Now apply what you have read about how to use positive reinforcers when you wish a behavior to continue, and then select a better answer.

[2b] You chose **he has never learned to wait.**

You are a good detective. But figuring out the cause does not help you know what to do about the situation. Your deduction must shed some light on the kind of action that might solve the problem. Turn back to the situation on page 22, and apply what you have learned about changing behavior so that you can select a better answer.

[2c] You chose **you did not reinforce the behavior you wished him to continue.**

EXCELLENT! If a child is anxious to speak and he gets to do it when he interrupts, but not when he waits, what do you expect him to do?

You need to recognize his effort and give him a turn to speak the first time he waits, to be sure he will repeat the action that works for him. "Bill, you are waiting so politely, let's give you a turn to talk right now." Obviously, you cannot always acknowledge him the minute he wants something, but you will find out how to deal with that situation later in this book. Now turn to page 25, and continue reading.

[2d] You chose **he is angry because you did not listen to him.**

No doubt. But you are angry, too, because you have had to put up with his behavior for a long time. This is the first time it has ever happened to him. Nevertheless, he tried being polite and waited when he wanted to speak, and that good behavior got him nowhere. Turn back to the question on page 22, and apply what you have read about changing behavior so his effort to do better will be reinforced.

WHAT ABOUT BEDTIME?

Bedtime is difficult for most parents. The child is tired, the parent is tired, and neither of you is at his best. When a child is fatigued, you cannot expect the same disposition and rationality from him that you would normally demand or that he would usually display. You must remember that you, too, will have less tolerance.

Because you are an adult *you know* you are tired and less patient. That is why it falls on you to compensate for this temporary factor in yourself. You do not want to sacrifice all you may have gained by suddenly reinforcing the wrong acts merely because you are weary.

The time for bed often becomes the evening issue between parents and children. But worn-out parents and tired children are in no condition for wise decision-making. Consequently, the time for bed should be set previously, when both parties are in better shape for negotiation. You can avoid many tearful scenes by having prior arrangements with your child about bedtime. Hopefully, parents will indicate some acceptable bedtime limits, and the child, as soon as he is old enough, will select the precise time on the clock.

You might introduce this notion by using a technique like this: "Johnny, boys your age should have twelve hours sleep. That means you must get to bed between 7:30 and 8:00. Now, you may decide the time between 7:30 and 8:00 that you want to go to bed." Letting Johnny be somewhat in charge of his fate by making this minor decision helps him accept your conditions.

Most children will decide on the latest possible time, so be sure when you set your limits that any time within them is acceptable to you. Once bedtime is set, except in a case of emergency, STICK TO IT! Be sure to *positively reinforce* the behavior of going to bed without a fuss, so that it will reoccur. ("You are certainly grown-up in the way you go to bed.")

Many parents do not realize that even children who can tell time are not *time conscious,* and may need to be reminded night after night. "Johnny, you decided that 8:00 was bedtime, so you have ten more minutes." This kind of warning helps a child to become aware of what time it is, and avoids some of the resentment he will feel if there is an unanticipated interruption for bedtime when he is in the middle of a fascinating activity. Older children can be asked pleasantly, "Do you know what time it is? How many minutes do you have before bedtime?" This approach not only helps their behavior, but their arithmetic as well.

Again, you must remember that our examples are merely illustrative, not a recipe for exactly what you should do or say. You need to tailor your own choice of comments to each situation, to the age of your child, and to the needs of your family.

AND THEN THERE IS DAWDLING

Dawdling before bedtime is one of the most effective methods of torturing parents ever devised by children. A generalized remedy to combat dawdling is to plan that the child's bath, brushing of teeth, and other pre-bedtime activities are completed well in advance of the specified bedtime. This tends to take away the temptation to dawdle, because even the younger child soon realizes he is using up his own free time rather than delaying bedtime if he chooses to dawdle.

Older children use the more sophisticated device of *remembering* they had homework. Again, creating time for all essential activities well in advance of bedtime circumvents the same delaying action on the part of older children. In any case, it is essential that you do not fall for the ruse.

While it will be difficult for you as a conscientious parent to withstand the *homework undone* situation, your steadfastness will pay dividends. ("You'll simply have to explain to your teacher that you forgot.") Going to school unprepared one time will help your child remember for the rest of the year. We might add that educators heartily endorse this approach. They wish parents would leave the homework task completely up to the child, for it is his job, not Mother's or Dad's.

Younger children also use the stratagem of bouncing back out of bed as many times as you will tolerate. They will announce that they need a drink, or must tell you something important that they forgot, or have a feeling they are still hungry. All these are ruses that you will positively reinforce and thereby encourage if you let them work.

As you have now learned, any undesirable acts that you positively reinforce (that get the child what he wants) will increase in their frequency of occurrence. Letting your child know that ruses won't work (and meaning it) is the only way to **extinguish** this behavior. If you say, "I'm sorry, try to remember it tomorrow night before you go to bed," you have thwarted the success of the ruse.

Parents often find this type of plea hard to resist, but we know of no child who has died of hunger or thirst as a result of not being able to get up out of bed after being tucked in. If you can't stand the thought of your parched child, put a glass of water at his bedside.

TIME OUT FOR SITUATIONS

As we have said before, accepting good behavior and *not* rewarding it with praise, privileges, or whatever a child needs or desires (in other words, forgetting positive reinforcers when the child behaves well) is a common error with most parents.

Let us try some fresh situations and see what you would do about them. We want to be sure that you will feel thoroughly comfortable with this new skill you are learning. We also want to be sure that you remember to reinforce your child's good behavior. Please run through the four practice situations that follow. Does any one of them sound like something that might happen at your house?

THREE

Your four-year-old child and you have agreed that when the little hand is here (marked on the clock with a color, picture, or a dot to indicate a time hopefully selected by the child) and the big hand points straight up, it is time for bed. Bath and toothbrushing have been finished. You have let the child choose whether he would like to play or be read to in the intervening time before bedtime. You have given the child a five-minute reminder that it is now time for bed. You have been a perfect parent, so you put the child to bed and say:

[a] **"Now stay there and do not get up."**_____turn to page 29, top.

[b] **"Tomorrow night I'll have to do something nice with you before bedtime because you are so good about going to bed."**

_____turn to page 29, bottom.

[c] **"Good night."**_____turn to page 30, top.

[d] **"Have a good sleep because tomorrow morning we are going to do something special."**_____turn to page 30, bottom.

[3a] You chose **"Now stay there and do not get up."**

Get up? What an inviting possibility, especially if the child had not already thought of it. Maybe he should try it out to see what would happen. No—at this point do not mention getting up. Turn back to the situation on page 28, and select an answer that would not suggest something you do not want to happen.

[3b] You chose **"Tomorrow night I will have to do something nice with you before bedtime because you are so good about going to bed."**

RIGHT! You are really understanding reinforcement theory. "Something nice" that is going to happen and being praised are reinforcers to almost all of us. Being told he is good and something nice is going to happen tomorrow night will increase the probability that he will go to bed on time again. But be sure that, when you say something nice is going to happen tomorrow night, *it really does*. That way he knows he can depend on you. The next night you need to remind him, "Remember that you did such a good job of going to bed last night, I said I would do something nice? What would you like it to be? A story, a dish of ice cream, playing games?" That night, when he goes to bed, you again positively reinforce the behavior you want to continue. "You always go to bed so well! Let us plan a special time just for you," or "I am glad you are my boy," or whatever would be appropriate to this situation. Later, we will explain why you do not have to continue this the rest of his life. Turn now to page 31.

[3c] You chose **"Good night."**

It would not be—a good night, that is. What is positively reinforcing about that statement? We do not think you really chose this response. You are only reading it to see what we have to say. You are right, it would not do the trick at all. Turn back to the situation on page 28. Choose an answer that you really believe in.

[3d] You chose **"Have a good sleep because tomorrow we are going to do something special."**

It might work, but we doubt it. What is the "something special"? If your four-year-old has any enterprise at all, he will get up and pursue the subject. At best, he will stay in bed and his mind will begin entertaining various possibilities, which is certainly not conducive to relaxation and sleep. No, you might just as well have plugged him into an electric current. Turn back to the situation on page 28, and select an answer that will leave him in a relaxed, satisfied state.

FOUR

Little Susy does not like vegetables, so she will not eat them.
You get her to take a taste and say:

[a] **"You see, they are really good."**_____turn to page 32, top.

[b] **"You see, they are not so bad."**_____turn to page 32, bottom.

[c] **"Now take another bite."**_____turn to page 33, top.

[d] **"Good girl! Here's a bite of**_____*(something she really likes)."*
_____turn to page 33, bottom.

[4a] You chose **"You see, they are really good."**

That is your opinion, but it may not be hers. You may be teaching her that different people like different things. But that is not increasing her desire to take a bite of vegetable. Turn back to the situation on page 31, and choose an answer where positive reinforcement will increase the probability that she will take another bite of vegetable.

[4b] You chose **"You see, they are not so bad."**

She may find the taste even worse than she expected, in which case there is no point in pretending it is not so. As a result, she will be even less inclined to eat any more. Turn back to the situation on page 31, and select an answer where your use of positive reinforcement will increase the probability that she will take another bite of vegetable.

[4c] You chose **"Now take another bite."**

Why should she? The first bite only got her a dose of what she did not want to do in the first place, which was eat her vegetable. If she does take another bite, who knows what other undesirable ideas you may get? Turn back to the situation on page 31, and select an answer where what you do will increase the probability that she will try another bite of vegetables.

[4d] You chose **"Good girl! Here is a bite of**_____
(something she really likes)."

CORRECT. You are giving her two positive reinforcers, your praise and a taste of something she likes. As a result, she will be more likely to try another bite of vegetable. This does not mean that by magic she will now like vegetables and beg for them, but if you continue to praise her for eating them and reward her with things she likes to eat, it will be highly likely that she will continue to eat vegetables and will surely develop a taste for some of them.

FiVE

Ten-year-old Bill typically complains he is too full to finish the nutritious part of his dinner, especially his salad, but when it is time for dessert his appetite magically returns. You wish him to develop good eating habits, to say nothing of making sure he gets the necessary vitamins and minerals. As a result, you:

[a] Tell him if he does not clean his plate, he cannot have dessert_____turn to page 35, top.

[b] Deliver a lecture on the value of vitamins_turn to page 35, bottom.

[c] Tell him if he does not eat the right food he will get sick_____turn to page 36, top.

[d] With his first bite of salad, you say. "Good for you, Bill! No wonder you are getting so strong and can do so many things!"
_____turn to page 36, bottom.

[5a] You chose **tell him if he does not clean his plate he cannot have dessert.**

The results of this will depend on how large a mound of undesirable food he has on his plate and what you have for dessert. The latter may not be worth the effort. Also, if he does eat the disliked salad, it will be with a *got-to-get-it-over-with* attitude which is not conducive to developing a liking for it. Even if the dessert is so luscious that it works this time, what about a time when dessert is mediocre (we all have those meals) or when there is no dessert at all (we all have those days, too)? Turn back to the situation on page 34, and select an answer that provides positive reinforcement at the moment he is engaged in the behavior you want him to continue.

[5b] You chose **deliver a lecture on the value of vitamins.**

If that works, for goodness sake publish your lecture, and we will all use it. Usually children could not care less about vitamins and are indifferent to their presence or absence in their daily fare. Possibly you will wind up in an argument ("How come Eskimos are healthy, *they* don't eat salads?") And add further unpleasantness to a meal that is already going on the rocks. Turn back to the situation on page 34, and select an answer that will make the meal more pleasant and increase the probability that Bill will continue to eat salad.

[5c] You chose **tell him if he does not eat the right food he will get sick.**

Unfortunately, there is too long a time span between cause and effect for him to be convinced. Unless he really understands physiology and nutrition, he will point out all his friends who do not eat salad and "they are not sick!" While we hope he is learning which foods build a healthy boy, *mealtime is not the time for formal instruction periods.* Turn back to the situation on page 34, and select an answer that will positively reinforce the behavior you want to continue.

[5d] You chose **with his first bite of salad, you say, "Good for you, Bill! No wonder you are getting so strong and can do so many things."**

THAT IS RIGHT! You were alert to the power of immediate positive reinforcement of behavior the moment it occurs. At this point in his life, Bill may eat salad only to get praised about being strong. There is a good chance that by eating what is good for him and being positively reinforced, he will develop a taste for it and eventually be reinforced by his own enjoyment of the food. But if he never eats his salad or always has an argument about eating it, we can almost guarantee he will never learn to like it.

SIX

Because mealtime presents so many problems to most parents, let us try another example with an older child.

Your teen-ager needs to pass up *gooey* desserts because of weight or acne. We hope you would provide appropriate light desserts or fruit so he would not be constantly tempted. At those times when a *gooey* dessert is unavoidably available, you can help your youngster's willpower by:

[a] A lecture on the evils of rich desserts_____turn to page 38, top.

[b] Forbidding the consumption of the dessert
_____turn to page 38, bottom.

[c] Saying it is up to him_____turn to page 39, top.

[d] Commenting on how well he has already done with face or figure and how great he looks_____turn to page 39, bottom.

[6a] You chose **a lecture on the evils of rich desserts.**

You will have joined a majority group, for that is all most parents ever do. The fact that the fattest and most pimply people also deliver that lecture should be ample evidence that it does not work. Talking about how bad something is usually does not deter people from indulging: witness tobacco, alcohol, and narcotics. Turn back to the situation on page 37, and select an answer that should have more influence on your adolescent's behavior.

[6b] You chose **forbidding the consumption of the dessert.**

That is one sure way of making it more desirable, to say nothing of inviting a challenging tug-of-war of the "I will"—"You will not" variety or, worse yet, surreptitious consumption of the forbidden dessert. Your determination that the dessert should not be consumed is admirable, but your action is unwise. Turn back to the situation on page 37, and select an answer that will be more apt to accomplish your objective.

[6c] You chose **saying it is up to him.**

You are wise enough to recognize the reality of the situation; it really *is* up to him. But our guess is that he would still appreciate a little assistance from you. Willpower is always easier to manifest if we have a little help and can feel noble while exercising it. Turn back to the situation on page 37, and select an answer that will assist him to make a decision to forgo the dessert.

[6d] You chose **commenting on how well he has already done with face or figure and how great he looks.**

THAT IS RIGHT. You are positively reinforcing the fact that he has not yet taken the dessert and, after your comment, he probably will not. It is easier to resist temptation after an observation that helps you focus on the fact that you are on the way to your goal and the results are becoming to your appearance. Think how much easier it is for *you* to diet after someone has just commented on your still youthful waistline. Turn now to page 40.

CHAPTER III

NEGATIVE REINFORCEMENT

It is unfortunate that all parents seem to see what their child is doing wrong more often than they see what he is doing right.

You notice the one dirty sock that remains on the floor—and never see that all the rest of the room is in order. You do not do or say something positive when your child is doing well. Instead, you often only DO SOMETHING when you see something wrong. This response is unfortunate and discouraging to your child.

But even more importantly, the SOMETHING that you DO when you are complaining or reprimanding your child will often have very different effects on his behavior from the effects you want or expect.

This special reaction of *any* individual (not just your child) to reprimand or punishment has now been studied extensively by psychologists and explained as **negative reinforcement.**

A negative reinforcer is anything unpleasant or not desired by your youngster. A negative reinforcer suppresses the behavior it immediately follows. When undesirable behavior is suppressed by a negative reinforcer, whatever behavior takes away that negative reinforcer is strengthened and we say that negative reinforcement has taken place.

& PUNISHMENT

Do you recall that we said earlier in this book that a positive reinforcer strengthens the behavior it immediately follows? You know that a positive reinforcer is something your child wants or likes. You also know that a negative reinforcer is something that your child does NOT want or does NOT like.

Negative reinforcement sounds like it is only the other side of the coin, doesn't it? Well, it does not quite work that way. *The effects of negative reinforcement on your child's behavior are not simply the reverse of positive reinforcement.* Negative reinforcement often has complicated results. That is why its effects on behavior are not always what we want or expect.

REALLY UNDERSTANDING NEGATIVE REINFORCEMENT

By understanding as much as you can about negative reinforcement you prevent unwanted results in your child's behavior. How ideal it would be if you could just *avoid* negative reinforcers, once you realize that positive reinforcement is generally the strongest and most direct tool to use in improving your child's behavior! But you get tired—you get angry—or you lose your perspective in some other way—and you

41

get carried away with using negative reinforcement in your dealings with your son or daughter.

So understanding how negative reinforcement works is the only safe answer. The first thing to remember is that a negative reinforcer *suppresses* the behavior it immediately follows. When undesirable behavior is held back by a negative reinforcer, *any behavior which removes the negative reinforcer is strengthened*—so we say that negative reinforcement has taken place. You will find, as we examine negative reinforcement further, that its effect on behavior can show up in two ways (often during the same incident):

[1] Negative reinforcement suppresses the behavior that brought on the negative reinforcer;

[2] Negative reinforcement strengthens any behavior that takes away the negative reinforcer.

If that seems confusing, do not give up! No one gets it on the first reading. Let us try an example.

Suppose that Johnny is acting in a silly fashion during dinner and suddenly knocks over his glass, spilling milk all over your clean tablecloth. Dad yells at him and Johnny begins to cry.

Dad's yelling (negative reinforcer) will suppress the silliness for the rest of the meal. The silliness that resulted in the careless spilling, however, is only suppressed for the time being. At another dinner, when Johnny has forgotten the episode, his carelessness will return. And so will Dad's yelling. However, if you are like most parents, Johnny's crying response will make Dad stop yelling and return to his normal voice.

But for Johnny it does not end there. When Johnny's crying takes away the negative reinforcer of Dad's yelling, the behavior of crying will be strengthened in Johnny. So he will learn to cry whenever anyone is annoyed or angry with him.

42

And what happened to the silliness? Not much! Johnny's crying behavior has been strengthened by taking away the negative reinforcer of yelling. But the silliness-at-the-table behavior has only been suppressed —it has *not* been eliminated—and we know that is not at all what Dad intended. This does not mean, however, that Dad should continue yelling to avoid strengthening Johnny's crying behavior.

What could Dad have done differently?

Let us look at this same example in two diagrams that show the main effects negative reinforcement can have on behavior.

First, we said negative reinforcement suppresses the behavior that brings on the negative reinforcer:

A ——→ brings on ——→ B ——→ which suppresses ——→ A

(silliness)   (yelling)   (silliness)

Next, we said negative reinforcement strengthens behavior that takes away the negative reinforcer:

C ——→ takes away ——→ B ——→ which strengthens ——→ C

(crying)   (yelling)   (crying in order
to take away an
adult's anger)

ANOTHER WAY OF EXPLAINING IT

It is important for you to realize that the same effect of negative reinforcement will occur whenever anything unpleasant happens, whether it is Dad yelling (at Johnny, or Mom, or his boss!) or the dog biting you, or a pair of shoes hurting you.

Let us take an adult story that shows the same principle at work. Suppose you have a tight pair of tan shoes. When you wear them, they hurt (negative reinforcement). Since you naturally want to get rid of hurting, you want to take them off the minute you put them on. The urge to take them off (the behavior that takes away the hurting) is strengthened. Even if taking off your shoes may not be appropriate, many times you slip your feet out of them whenever you can.

Every time you want to wear your tan suit you look at those tan shoes. You do not want to put them on. Putting on the tan shoes is the behavior that brings on the hurt (negative reinforcer), so that behavior is being suppressed. Negative reinforcement (the hurting) is suppressing the behavior of putting on the shoes, because that behavior brought on the hurting (negative reinforcement).

But it does not end there. Let us take the shoe problem a step further. The hurting discourages you from wearing the tan shoes, but if you wear the tan suit what shoes should you wear? The reddish brown? The black ones? *The negative reinforcement of the hurt has given you absolutely no information about what you should do.* You know only what you should *not* do.

It is important to stop here and realize that *negative reinforcement tells a child what he should not do but does not give your child any information about what he should actually do.* Like the tan shoes, the negative reinforcement tells the child only what will bring on pain. It does not provide constructive guidance about what he should do to get a comfortable response.

Going back to the problem of what to do about the tan shoes: Perhaps you try wearing your black ones with the tan suit. They are comfortable, and you get through the day with physical ease. But you experience some mental anguish, because you wonder if the black shoes and the tan suit really look well together.

The next time you wear the tan suit, you try your reddish brown shoes, which are equally comfortable. This time you receive a number of compliments. "What good looking shoes!"—"Are they Cordovan?"—"They look awfully expensive!"—"They really look good with that suit." are the remarks you hear throughout the day. So what will you do next time you put on that suit? Pretty obvious, isn't it?

Did you notice that *all the positive reinforcers* about the reddish brown shoes *tell you what to do?* Negative reinforcement (hurting) established what you should *not* do (wear the tan shoes). But it did not give you information about what you should do. Assuming the other shoes were equally comfortable, you probably would have taken turns with them until the compliments (positive reinforcers) strengthened one of your choices and made it more likely to reoccur.

Notice the words "more likely." The reinforced behavior is not guaranteed forever (you may decide to try the black shoes again or buy a new pair of tan ones). The positively reinforced behavior is simply more probable (most of the time you will choose the reddish brown shoes). Moreover, the larger the number of favorable comments (positive reinforcers) that you receive on the reddish brown shoes, the more likely you are to wear them without feeling inclined to try something else.

BACK TO YOUR CHILDREN

You may not have been aware of it, but as a parent you have had many of your own behaviors toward your child shaped by negative reinforcement. For example, your child crying in the crib was a negative reinforcer (something you did not want to hear). You picked him up and the crying stopped (your behavior took away the negative reinforcer). Your response of picking him up was strengthened because it removed his crying. Often you did not want to put him down for fear the crying would start again—so your putting him down was suppressed. But remember that your child's own crying behavior was also strengthened, because it was positively reinforced (you picked him up). So, whenever your child wanted to be picked up, he knew what to do.

Often crying and being picked up becomes a vicious circle. The child cries to be picked up. Parents pick the child up because they do not want to hear the crying. The response of parents that stops the crying (picking child up) is strengthened by negative reinforcement because it did stop the crying (which is a negative reinforcer to the parents). The trouble is, you do not want crying behavior to be strengthened in your child if it merely expresses a child's fussing.

But, on the other hand, you *do* want crying behavior to be strengthened if the child does it to let you know when something is really wrong. The trick is to be able to tell the difference between types of crying so that you strengthen appropriate signals for help from your child and you weaken fussing behavior.

Let us look at another example of negative reinforcement in a family situation. But a word of caution: Remember that all these instances are only examples, never *what-you-must-do* recipes.

Here is the example. Diane often drums with her fingers while you are talking. As a result she may not really hear what you are saying and you, quite certainly, are irritated. You decide to negatively reinforce (suppress) the drumming behavior by stopping in the middle of a sentence and looking sternly at her whenever she starts to drum.

The unexpected silence causes the whole family to focus on what stopped you from speaking (Diane's drumming). Your silence and all the eyes on her are uncomfortable (negative reinforcers) to Diane. She stops drumming and starts listening, so you resume your speaking.

Your immediate negative reinforcement (silence and a look) has affected Diane's behavior (drumming) in two ways:

[1] It suppressed the behavior that brought on the negative reinforcement (Diane does not drum because you will give her "the look");

[2] It strengthened the behavior (her listening) that took the negative reinforcement away (you stopped looking and started talking).

In this hypothetical situation you have used both steps in negative reinforcement to change the response that it immediately follows. You have (1) suppressed the response (drumming) that brings on the negative reinforcer *(the look),* and you have (2) strengthened the desirable response (Diane listening) that takes away the negative reinforcer *(the look).* You have used negative reinforcement to suppress Diane's inattention to you on this particular occasion. Now, if you move in with positive reinforcement when she is paying attention ("Diane, you are such a good listener. I have to say it only once!") you have it made!

And be sure to *continue* the positive reinforcement when Diane listens politely in the future, so that you increase the chances of improving her behavior permanently.

MAKING IT ALL MORE CLEAR

One of the problems of using any negative reinforcer is that you may not always be aware of the action that *takes away* the negative reinforcer. You may not, therefore, be sure which particular behavior is being strengthened—and it could be something you do not wish to strengthen. On the other hand, when you use positive reinforcers, you can pinpoint exactly the behavior that is being affected.

Suppose you give your child a special treat when he cleans his room. Cleaning his room is the behavior that is being strengthened. But

47

suppose, instead, you punish him if he does not clean it. Then you have to worry about the fact that any behavior that removes punishment will be strengthened.

You intend that the behavior to be strengthened is room cleaning. But in actual fact it could be any one of the following that might make us relent and remove the punishment:

[1] **Sobbing as if his heart were broken**

[2] **Arguing that you are not fair because his brother made the mess**

[3] **Getting a stomach ache**

[4] **Stuffing everything under the bed**

[5] **Remembering he has homework**

[6] **Having a temper tantrum that will distract you**

[7] **Redirecting your attention by such questions as "Where did I come from?"**

Obviously you do not wish to strengthen any of these or similar behaviors. But if any of them accidentally works for your child—watch out! That behavior will happen again, because you have strengthened it through negative reinforcement.

The difference between positive and negative reinforcement may become clearer with the following diagrams.

BEHAVIOR WE WANT	REINFORCER	BEHAVIOR WE GET
Room cleaning	Positive: reward for cleaning	Room cleaning
	Negative: punishment for not cleaning	Any of the following:
		1. possibly room cleaning *but more likely*
		2. sobbing as if his heart is broken
		3. arguing that you are not fair because his brother made the mess
		4. getting a stomach ache
		5. stuffing everything under the bed
		6. remembering he has homework
		7. having a temper tantrum that will distract you
		8. redirecting your attention ("Where did I come from?")

Avoiding sweets before dinner	Positive: an extra goodie *after* dinner	Not eating sweets before dinner
	Negative: punishment for eating	Any of the following:
		1. possibly not eating sweets before dinner *but more likely*
		2. sneaking sweets
		3. lying
		4. going to neighbor to get them
		5. whining and wheedling
		6. tantrums
		7. trying to negotiate
		8. "You just don't love me!"

BEHAVIOR WE WANT	REINFORCER	BEHAVIOR WE GET
Doing his homework	Positive	Finished homework
	Negative	Any of the following:
		1. possibly finished homework *but more likely*
		2. slopping through carelessly
		3. getting a headache
		4. crying
		5. copying when he should not
		6. cheating
		7. saying it is done when it is not
		8. losing the assignment
		9. destroying paper so he cannot finish

SUMMARY

Negative reinforcement strengthens the behavior that takes away the negative reinforcer. This means that undesirable behaviors can be strengthened if they take away punishment. For example: When cheating or lying takes away punishment, when daydreaming takes away attending to work, when telling a lie takes away consequences, all of these undesirable behaviors are being strengthened. This is why negative reinforcement can cause problems through unwanted effects.

NOW FOR A LOOK AT PUNISHMENT

If you can wipe your mind clean of all bias about rearing children the subject of punishment will be easier to understand. It is extremely important that punishment be understood for what it can do as well as what it cannot do. *Punishment is a negative reinforcer,* and the trouble begins right there.

This may sound as if it does not present much of a problem, but let us take a look at some of the possibilities: Telling a lie can take away punishment. Cheating can take away (the punishment of) losing a game. Pretending to be sick can take away (the punishment of) an unpleasant task. Undesirable behaviors will be strengthened the minute that one of them works and results in the removal of a punishment. If your child has any of these problems, it is probably because that was the undesirable behavior that worked in the past to get him out of an unpleasant situation.

Because *negative reinforcers strengthen whatever takes them away,* negative reinforcers are dangerous in the same way a sharp knife is dangerous. In the hands of a bumblefingers, someone can get hurt. In the hands of a surgeon, a sharp knife can save a life. We must be skilled to use punishment wisely. Unfortunately, punishment may suppress irritating behavior for the time being. This tempts you to use it. The complexities and undesirable results of punishment are not always evident until you fail to get the results you expect from it. Then you find that to do something unpleasant is not enough.

The *something* that you *do* may actually be better left undone, judging by the results. Remember how Dad's yelling unintentionally strengthened Johnny's crying behavior when what Dad wanted was to stop Johnny from spilling things at the table? While you may wish your child to experience the undesirable consequences of his actions, do not forget that punishment is a negative reinforcer that can actually strengthen undesirable behavior.

When you use positive reinforcement you know the particular behavior that is being strengthened. But in negative reinforcement you often cannot control the action that takes away the punishment. You are not sure which behavior is being strengthened. You always need to remember the dangers of punishment in negative reinforcement—even though punishment may sometimes be necessary.

Yes, that is true! *Punishment may sometimes be necessary.* You have to suppress behavior that is dangerous or hurtful—you cannot just hope your child will grow out of it. But you need to think it through carefully. You need to look ahead to see what the punishment will or will not accomplish. The moment you use punishment as a negative reinforcer you must carefully watch for what removes the punishment. You must be sure the removal of the punishment is associated with a behavior you want strengthened in your child.

Remember, a negative reinforcer only suppresses a behavior. It will not eliminate it, nor will it tell the child how to act instead.

For example, the child may stop hitting his little brother if he knows he will get a spanking. But what should he do the next time, when that same little brother has taken his belongings or wrecked something that belonged to him? How does a spanking teach the child appropriate ways of dealing either with his little brother or with his legitimate feelings of anger? It is just as important for the child to learn how to deal with frustrating situations as to learn to suppress the violence that frustration stirs inside him!

The spanking obviously does nothing but cause him to suppress a behavior his parents did not like. Again, we see that punishment will teach the child what to stop doing, but not what to do in its place. *Punishment never does more than part of the job.* You must do the other part by teaching your child what he should do in place of the undesirable behavior, and then positively reinforce him when he does behave the way you want him to.

USING PUNISHMENT PROPERLY

Punishment used often and indiscriminately is ineffective and can do

lasting damage. But punishment that is based on reasonable consequences for misbehavior and used judicially by a wise parent is another
matter. Such punishment can suppress undesirable behavior and open
the way to positive reinforcement, so your child can be taught a more
desirable way of acting.

However, parents commit so many unintentional *sins* when they
punish their children that the decision to punish should be considered
very carefully.

[1] What will this punishment accomplish?

Our child's undesirable behavior will be suppressed, we hope.

[2] What will this (or any other) punishment not accomplish?

*Punishment will not teach a child what he should do in place of what
he did that got him punished.* He may only substitute another undesirable behavior in place of the first.

[3] What will punishment do that you do not want to happen?

The child may become resentful, or he may learn to become deceitful
to avoid the punishment. As a normal reaction to being punished he
may want to retaliate, but because he doesn't dare, he hits a younger
brother or sister instead. You are not immune to undesirable reactions
from punishing your child, either. You probably have guilt feeling and
fear that you will lose your child's love because he doesn't understand
words like, "This hurts me more than it does you," and "I'm doing this
for your own good."

One of the best ways to avoid a punishment that misfires is to make sure your child thinks it is fair. You might let him have a part in deciding what the consequences should be if something forbidden has been done. "You help us decide what should happen the next time you come in late" (or hit your sister, or speak rudely, or whatever the unacceptable behavior is).

Deciding with your child what the consequences will be if he does a forbidden act is more effective than physical punishment. Now is a good time to see why this is true. Consider the alternatives.

Physical punishment usually is an act of anger completely unrelated to the misbehavior. For this reason slapping and spanking (and even yelling) usually accomplish little more than draining off parental anger. Something more carefully thought out and agreed upon with your child, like giving up his allowance, giving up the privilege of buying toys or candy to pay for something he has broken, being *grounded* because he left without permission, or going to his room when he is disagreeable to others, are normal consequences that occur throughout life and might as well be learned now.

This approach usually results in more effective behavior change than any number of angry lectures or severe actions inflicted by an irate parent. More importantly, agreeing on consequences places part of the responsibility on the youngster, where it rightfully belongs. You may find yourself amazed at the ability of even a two- or three-year-old to help set his own consequences, although for young children you may need to suggest alternatives like, "What do you think will help you remember not to do that? Should you stay in your room until dinner, or give up your_____ (something he likes) for today?"

ONE LAST CAUTION

Punishment is a specific type of negative reinforcer, for it is something that we deliberately do to our child as a result of some action of his. It is different from many negative reinforcers in that it is consciously inflicted by one person on another. It is unlike normal negative reinforcers such as your shoe hurting, or a stove burning your finger.

Let us look at an example of this difference. Suppose you tell your child not to touch a pan because it is hot. He disobeys, touches the pan, and is burned. He has been negatively reinforced by the burn, but he has not been punished. If, in addition to being burned, he is sent to his room because he disobeyed you, then he has been punished.

It is important for you to keep this distinction in mind. Since punishment of all kinds is a negative reinforcer that is consciously inflicted by one person on another, physical punishment should be considered even more soberly.

Because so many of us fall unintentionally into this habit, special attention needs to be given to such physical punishments as slapping, shaking, or spanking. Occasionally it is necessary to stop behavior by physical means, and it is possible for a spanking to clear the air so that everyone can start over. If it happens very often, however, this type of punishment loses its effectiveness, and *usually generates more resentment than change of behavior.*

Like other negative reinforcers, physical punishment (spanking, shaking, slapping) and other severe forms of punishment ("Stay in your room for the whole day!" or "You can't have the car for six months!") may actually give rise to undesirable results that we had not bargained for. So you must try to anticipate any unexpected or dangerous effects when you are deciding whether or how much to punish your child, and avoid them as best you can.

On the other hand, punishment can become so routine that neither parent nor child is putting any thoughtful effort into changing the undesirable behavior that caused the punishment. Slap-him-and-forget-it can become a habit. This is because punishment that happens often may come to be ignored altogether and thus become useless.

Remember, a negative reinforcer only suppresses a behavior. It will not eliminate it. It is important to know how and when to use it, *sparingly and wisely.* It is also essential that you always keep in mind the behavior that you want to replace the undesirable behavior, so you can teach that good behavior and *positively reinforce* it when it occurs.

LOOKING AT SOME SAMPLE SITUATIONS

It is essential that you *identify desirable behavior* to replace the undesirable behavior. Then you must help the child to behave in the desirable way (telling the truth, getting the job done). Finally you must positively reinforce that behavior. This is the only way you can be sure that some undesirable behavior (cheating, falsifying, withdrawing) that takes away the negative reinforcer is not inadvertently being strengthened.

Fortunately there are many standard situations in the home that you can think about in advance of their occurrence. In these situations you know only too well the undesirable behavior that you want to suppress. But you need to discover exactly what desirable behavior you want to replace the misbehavior that we are seeking to suppress.

This will not be a simple task. The examples in this book will help you to perfect your skill. If you feel that you understand the theory of negative reinforcement, you will not need to read through all of the examples. Just glance at the situation described in the box and if you think it does not apply to your child, go on to one that does.

Shall we begin?

SEVEN

When your child has been fooling around during his meal, you may have tried the technique of keeping him at the table until he is finished. To most children who would like to be excused, this is a negative reinforcer. Which behavior do you wish to suppress by negative reinforcement?

[a] **Not taking mealtime seriously** —————————turn to page 58, top.

[b] **Fooling around during meals** —————————turn to page 58, bottom.

[c] **Poor eating habits** —————————turn to page 59, top.

[d] **Not minding his parents** —————————turn to page 59, bottom.

[7a] You chose **not taking mealtime seriously.**

Of course you would like him to think meals are important, but unfortunately, or perhaps fortunately, not all of them are. If he were so serious that he chewed each mouthful fifteen times, he probably would not finish. He would still need to stay after the rest of the family is excused. Go back to the situation on page 57, and look for the specific behavior you want to suppress.

[7b] You chose **fooling around during meals.**

RIGHT YOU ARE! And about time you did something about it. Your disposition and the appearance of the tablecloth will improve. As long as he plays, he will never be able to devote his attention to the task at hand (eating with reasonable care). The sooner you suppress this behavior, the better. This is not to say that playing is not normal and to be expected, but society will not accept playing when he should be attending to what he is doing. Now turn to page 57.

[7c] You chose **poor eating habits.**

He may have poor eating habits all right, but this is a general trait and your negative reinforcer of keeping him at the table will suppress a more specific behavior. You cannot hope to redesign his whole outlook on food with such a specific punishment as keeping him at the table. Go back to the situation on page 57, and look for the specific behavior we want to suppress.

[7d] You chose **not minding his parents.**

It sounds like a desirable goal, but what if sometime you unintentionally make a mistake? Should he mind without question then? Besides, you do not know that he is deliberately disobeying. Maybe if you asked him why you were concerned about his actions, he would look at you blankly because he had not even thought about it; he was just enjoying himself. Go back to the situation on page 57, and look for a more specific behavior you want to suppress.

EiGHT

Now that you have established that the negative reinforcer of keeping a child at the table should suppress his playing during mealtime, what response are you strengthening? Negative reinforcement will strengthen the behavior that takes away the negative reinforcer of staying after the family is excused (remember taking off the shoes that hurt?). What will take away this negative reinforcer and thereby be the response that is strengthened?

[a] **Finishing his meal**———————————————turn to page 61, top.

[b] **Minding**————————————————————turn to page 61, bottom.

[c] **Taking his mealtime seriously**——————turn to page 62, top.

[d] **Having his other parent decide that he is not to be kept at the table**——————turn to page 62, bottom.

[8a] You chose **finishing his meal.**

THAT'S RIGHT. The minute he finishes, he is excused to go, and his staying at the table after the rest of the family has left is terminated. That is, unless you feel compelled to give him a moral lecture. If you do you will probably lose the ground gained by negative reinforcement. If you excuse him the minute he is finished, he should learn that if he does what he is supposed to do he will not have to stay after the others. Hopefully you will also positively reinforce his finishing with some praise or approval. Then he will do it again. Turn to page 63.

[8b] You chose **minding.**

Don't we wish it! But it is not as easy as that. Suppose he minded his manners and ignored his food. He would not be finished. Besides, if he eats like a pig, he could get done in time. Maddening, isn't it? You had better turn back to the situation on page 60, and choose an answer that is more likely to happen.

[8c] You chose **taking his mealtime seriously.**

Could be, but we cannot count on it. Plodding Peter, who eats slowly, may not finish, but Flashy Freddy can gulp it down in a few minutes. Think about what behavior took away the negative reinforcer of staying at the table. Then turn back to the situation on page 60, and make another choice.

[8d] You chose **having his other parent decide that he is not to be kept at the table.**

If you chose this, you and your spouse have some important discussion ahead of you, for the two of you are in a real mess. Quickly turn back to the question on page 60, and make another choice.

NINE

Now your child has had his behavior of playing during mealtime suppressed by the negative reinforcer of staying until he finishes, and has had his behavior of finishing his meal strengthened (it took away the negative reinforcer of staying at the table). What can you do to increase the probability that he will finish his meal next time? (If he had been smart enough to throw up, we would have let him leave the table too, wouldn't we?—but we wouldn't want that to happen again.) Think about what you have learned that will increase the probability of a correct response recurring.

[a] Point out to him the importance of finishing his meal————————————————turn to page 64, top.

[b] Calculate with him the amount of playtime he has missed————————————————turn to page 64, bottom.

[c] Show him how much of our time he has taken————————————————turn to page 65, top.

[d] Positively reinforce him for finishing his meal————————————————turn to page 65, bottom.

[9a] You chose **point out to him the importance of finishing his meal.**

How many times do you think this has happened to a child who does not finish? Obviously it is a useless technique or he would not still be having the problem. He has probably learned long ago to turn off his hearing aid when adults start to lecture. Go back to the situation on page 63, and select an answer to which he will listen.

[9b] You chose **calculate with him the amount of playtime he has missed.**

This might give him some arithmetic practice but we doubt it. The answer will probably confirm his suspicion that meals take too much time out of the more important aspects of the day, and so he may try to incorporate more play into mealtime. Go back to the situation on page 63, and select an answer that will increase his desire to attend to his eating.

[9c] You chose **show him how much of our time he has taken.**

Depending on what kind of a fiend he is, he may shout for joy. After all, you are taking his time with your silly insistence on eating. If he is truly sorry, all you have done is make him feel guilty, which will in no way help him attend to his meal. Go back to the situation on page 63, and select a better answer.

[9d] You chose **positively reinforce him for finishing his meal.**

CORRECT! That is what will increase the probability of finishing his next meal. If you say, "You're a good sport," or "I had no idea you could do so well. No wonder you're growing so strong," he is going to be more apt to finish his next meal to get some more praise. Of course, you tailor what you say and do to the needs and maturity of your child. The words you use with a five-year-old are insulting to a twelve-year-old. The theory is the same, however. Most people respond favorably to anything that makes them feel adequate and appreciated. You are a fast learner and are ready to turn to the next page.

Let us summarize what we have learned so far.

[1] If you want to strengthen a behavior, you positively reinforce it. When Bill's work is complimented by his father, his good work behavior is strengthened.

[2] If you want to suppress undesirable behavior you negatively reinforce it but are careful that desirable behavior takes away the negative reinforcer or punishment. If Bill's poor work earns him a scolding from his father, he could go to his room and pout. That would take away the scolding by avoiding his father, and pouting would be strengthened. If we want good work to be strengthened, Dad must stand by to see that Bill does a good job and then praise him for it.

[3] The crux of the whole matter is to see that your child does the right thing and then positively reinforce him. **Use negative reinforcement only to help you get him to do the right thing, never as his "just desserts!"**

CHAPTER IV
ELIMINATING UNDESIRABLE BEHAVIOR

When you read this chapter heading, did you puzzle over it a bit? Did you say to yourself, "I thought I just learned about eliminating undesirable behavior. What can this be about?"

Well, first you learned that positive reinforcers will increase the chances that your child's good behavior will occur over and over again. Next, you learned that negative reinforcers will suppress behavior that you do not want but that any behavior that makes the negative reinforcer go away will be strengthened.

As you have been working with these first two methods, you no doubt have eliminated many undesirable behaviors in your child by replacing them with behaviors that are better. Your main goal has been to see desirable behavior take root in your child. After all, that is what child rearing is all about.

Yet there are days when, harried and harrassed, you may also have asked, "Isn't there some method that won't reinforce *anything*, but will just make some of the dreadful behavior go away?"

Behavior is extinguished when it has no reinforcement whatsoever.
Put another way, we do not keep on doing something that gets abso-

lutely no reaction. When what we do fails to work in any way, we stop doing it.

TAKE THE CASE OF SALLY

Let us look at an imaginary child named Sally for an example of extinction. Sally has learned to fuss to get her way because it worked for her. As you would expect, she will continue to fuss as long as it gets her what she wants. But if Sally's parents decide to take no notice of her fussing and manage instead just to ignore it, eventually Sally will discard fussing as a means of getting her way because it doesn't work. Her fussing is extinguished. That is, provided her fussing behavior is not reinforced by Grandma, Uncle Harry, or other people.

Scolding or ridicule (both negative reinforcers) probably would cause Sally to suppress her fussing. But they would not cause Sally's fussing behavior to disappear. For that to happen, Sally would have to replace fussing with a desirable way of asking for things, a way that would get what she wants. But we know that Sally could not learn a desirable way of asking for what she wants from negative reinforcers 69 because, if you remember, no information about the right thing to do is provided by a negative reinforcer. A negative reinforcer only suppresses.

In extinction the behavior disappears even when you do not provide a substitute behavior. Sally may find a replacement behavior herself (crying or demanding) that you might also have to extinguish, so it is better to suggest a desirable way of asking.

The main hazard of negative reinforcement (strengthening *whatever* behavior takes away the negative reinforcer, whether such behavior is desirable or not) does not apply in extinction. But extinction may be a longer process. To suppress behavior that is dangerous to your child extinction may not be emphatic or swift enough ("Come away from that fire NOW!"). Resort to negative reinforcement in these cases, but watch out for its pitfalls.

What would positive reinforcement do for the fussing problem Sally has? Let us see how that method works *along with* extinction.

Say that you are extinguishing Sally's fussing behavior by ignoring it. When fussing does not work she may try asking for something pleasantly. You have been watching for this correct behavior, so you immediately reinforce it positively ("How nicely you asked. Of course you may go," or "Well, that isn't possible just now, but you were so good about not fussing that you may do——————————————— [something she wants] instead").

Sally has now demonstrated a new and better behavior. If you continue the positive reinforcement, Sally will more and more tend to repeat the behavior that you prefer. But if you ignore Sally's good behavior, you might actually extinguish the very behavior you want to promote. Extinction works on good behavior too and because you do not want that to happen you must remember to reinforce it positively.

From the examples given about the imaginary Sally, you can see
that in both positive and negative reinforcement something happens to

Sally as a direct result of her behavior. But to extinguish a behavior nothing must happen as the result of the behavior—it must have no reinforcement whatever.

Remembering that, let us look at some examples of how we might extinguish undesirable behavior. Read the situations in the boxes below and select your response, as you have done before.

TEN

Your four-year-old has just come out with his first (to your knowledge) *damn*. While playing with a group in a backyard building project, he said, "The damn truck won't work!" Obviously, you would like to extinguish that part of his vocabulary. What should you do?

[a] Be sure that he sees you looking horrified, but say nothing———————————turn to page 72, top.

[b] Take him to one side and explain that this is not appropriate language———————turn to page 72, bottom.

[c] Stop the play and give a resounding lecture on swearing—————————————turn to page 73, top.

[d] Act as if you had not heard it—————turn to page 73, bottom.

[10a.] You chose **be sure that he sees you looking horrified but say nothing.**

Horrifying an adult is one of the most fun things a little boy can do! If he can get you to react like that to such a simple situation, who knows to what vocabulary heights he might ascend if he really put his mind to it? Besides, as a result of his language, nothing has happened to him—just to you. You also run the risk that he thinks you are horrified with him, not his behavior. The obvious conclusion is that you don't like him. Go back to the question on page 71, and choose an answer that may extinguish his *damn*.

[10b] You chose **take him to one side and explain that this is not appropriate language.**

At least you have the sensitivity not to humiliate him in front of the group. Also, some members of the group may not have heard him and you are avoiding the undesirable possibility of teaching the word to those who may not know it. Nevertheless, if this is the first time the word has appeared, you are making too much of it. By doing so, you are insuring that he will remember the word. Go back to the question on page 71, and choose an answer that has a greater possibility of making him forget it.

[10c] You chose **stop the play and give a resounding lecture on swearing.**

You will accomplish one thing for sure. Everyone in the group will learn the word *damn*. They will also learn that it has the power of stopping whatever is going on and putting an adult in orbit. Do not be surprised (if you have an alert group) to hear *damn* again from several sources. Go back to the question on page 71, and choose an answer that will have the opposite effect.

[10d.] You chose **act as if you had not heard it.**

CORRECT. When such language tried for the first time produces no perceivable effect, it is apt to be dropped. Remember, a response is extinguished when it has no reinforcement whatsoever. We usually do not continue to do things that produce no results.

No one can guarantee that he will not say *damn* again. Maybe he will get a response from his playmates, or perhaps he has already had a reaction from an adult. (This is one reason many children swear.) In spite of this, you have chosen the most appropriate action for the first time you heard it. *Ignoring a response helps a child forget that response.* However, should he use the word again, you may need a negative reinforcer to suppress the response. *Negative reinforcement helps a child with an habitual response to remember what not to do.*

See the difference? Now turn to the next page.

ELEVEN

Your youngster has developed the habit of demanding what he wants and seems to have forgotten or has never learned the social amenities of *please* or *would you*. You are busy doing something and he has just set your disposition on edge by a strident "Hurry up and fix me something to eat." Rather than complying with his rude demand, you wisely decide to extinguish his behavior by:

[a] **A well-aimed blow**————————————turn to page 75, top.

[b] **Getting him a sandwich**————————turn to page 75, bottom.

[c] **Ignoring him and continuing what you are doing**————————————turn to page 76, top.

[d] **Telling him you will not do it unless he asks more politely**————————turn to page 76, bottom.

[11a] You chose **a well-aimed blow.**

If he does not duck and you make contact, you will probably be sorry. As a result of your guilt feeling, you may even get him something to eat. If you miss him, your annoyance will increase and who knows where it may all end? Hitting is a poor kind of negative reinforcer, so by all means extinguish that impulse. Turn back to the question on page 74, and choose an answer to extinguish your child's undesirable rudeness.

[11b] You chose **getting him a sandwich.**

You are a more tolerant parent than we are, and you will need to be because you are positively reinforcing his rudeness, thereby increasing the probability that it will happen again. This is no favor to him because other people will not react as you do, and his rudeness will get him in trouble. Turn back to the question on page 74, and select an answer that will extinguish his undesirable behavior.

[11c] You chose **ignoring him and continuing what you are doing.**

YES. We cannot think of a better way to extinguish his undesirable behavior. Doing nothing about feeding him makes it very clear that you're not going to be ordered around in that tone of voice, and you also are not descending to his level by starting an argument. Finding that rudeness gets him nowhere may help him remember his manners and he may ask for something to eat in an acceptable way. The moment he does, be sure to positively reinforce his polite request by feeding him immediately or by telling him you will just as soon as you can. That is one way he will learn to be polite. Once he has learned, you will not have to jump up every time he asks appropriately. You will learn what to do about that later in this book. Turn now to page 77.

[11d] You chose **telling him you will not do it unless he asks more politely.**

At least you have the wisdom not to reinforce his rudeness when he asks impolitely. But what if he says through his teeth, or in a mocking voice, "Mother dear, would you *please* get me something to eat?" then where are you? Probably at the beginning of an argument. There is a better way to extinguish his rudeness. Turn back to the question on page 74, and select an answer that will not get a rise out of you.

ELIMINATING ARGUING: ONE BEHAVIOR YOU WOULD LIKE TO GET RID OF

One behavior most parents would like to extinguish is arguing. Nothing is more tiresome than a contentious child who disputes every point, or a child who feels free to argue with your every request when you simply want to have your instructions accepted and obeyed. So arguing very often heads the list of behaviors we want to extinguish.

The really hard part is yours. It is unbelievably simple, if you remember that your first job is to extinguish any impulse you may have to argue. It takes two to argue. If you will not, your youngster cannot.

Approach the arguing child with a positive statement: "That's not the way I feel" or "I don't agree with you" or "I don't believe that is so" to make your position clear. Then meet all of his argumentative statements with *NO RESPONSE*. If he can't get a rise out of you his arguing probably will become extinguished. It may take more than one time but it will really work.

But be sure you really do ignore the statements your child dangles as bait to entice you into an argument, or you are sunk. Just one response, or even a look, lets your child know you are hooked and the arguing has been positively reinforced and will continue.

CONSIDER THESE EXAMPLES

Let us go back and look again at the difference between negative reinforcement and extinction. Negative reinforcement lets a child know what not to do.

For example, if he exhibits behavior such as hitting another child to get a toy, and you scold him (negative reinforcement), he knows he should not hit. The scolding suppresses the hitting, but still the child does not know an appropriate way to get the toy.

But if your child hits another child to get a toy and the other child ignores him (the other child does not hit back and he does not give up his toy), your child learns that hitting will not secure the toy. The hitting response has been extinguished because it produced no results.

Or perhaps your child does force some child to give him a toy by hitting him. In such a case, that behavior has been positively reinforced and your child will hit again when he wants something.

Let us examine a few examples of other kinds of behavior to understand negative reinforcement, positive reinforcement, and extinction.

TWELVE

12. Bob has learned to bully, so he threatens his brothers and sisters with physical harm if they do not let him have what he wants. They are afraid of him, so they let him have his way. His behavior of threatening others has been:

[a] **Positively reinforced**——————————turn to page 79, top.

[b] **Negatively reinforced**——————————turn to page 79, bottom.

[c] **Extinguished**——————————turn to page 80, top.

[12a] You chose **positively reinforced.**

WE'LL SAY IT HAS! It works so well that it will probably reoccur when-ever he wants the same thing or anything else. Now turn to page 81.

[12b] You chose **negatively reinforced.**

Unfortunately not, we wish it had been. Being a bully worked so well he will try it again. Turn back to the question on page 78, and select an answer that shows why his response of threatening will probably happen again when he wants his way.

[12c] You chose **extinguished.**

We wish it had been, but this only happens when threatening gets him no place. This threat got him what he wanted. Turn back to the question on page 78, and choose an answer that will explain why he probably will act in the same obnoxious way next time.

THIRTEEN

Let us suppose that this time Bob threatens his brothers and sisters and as a result his dad puts him in his room. His threatening has been:

[a] Positively reinforced———————————turn to page 82, top.

[b] Negatively reinforced———————————turn to page 82, bottom.

[c] Extinguished———————————turn to page 83, top.

[13a] You chose **positively reinforced.**

Thank goodness you are wrong! If it had been positively reinforced, it would be likely to happen again. His dad put him in his room so he would not be so apt to act that way again. Turn back to the question on page 81, and choose an answer that shows his threatening behavior has been suppressed.

[13b] You chose **negatively reinforced.**

RIGHT YOU ARE! Being put in his room is something he does not like so, hopefully, even though he wants to threaten his brothers and sisters, he will refrain from it or he will not get to play with them at all. The negative reinforcement (putting him in his room) has suppressed his threatening response, but he still may not know how he should act to get what he wishes. Do not think that just because you have told him what to do, he now knows. Learning new behavior patterns is not that simple. He must practice the appropriate behavior and be positively reinforced for it. Now turn to page 84.

[13c] You chose **extinguished.**

Unfortunately not. When his father is not there to put him in his room, he probably will return to his old bullying ways. Go back to the question on page 81, and choose an answer that shows his threatening has not been changed but only suppressed by the action of his father.

FOURTEEN

Now let us suppose that Bob begins to play with other children who are too big to be scared of him. Every time he threatens to hurt them if they do not let him have his way, they just ignore him and go on with the game. If he tries to hit one of the bigger boys, he is simply brushed off. His threatening is getting him nowhere so it is being:

[a] Positively reinforced————————————turn to page 85, top.

[b] Negatively reinforced————————————turn to page 85, bottom.

[c] Extinguished————————————————turn to page 86, top

[14a] You chose **positively reinforced.**

Again, thank goodness, it was not! It did not get him his way; it got him ignored. Go back to the question on page 84, and choose an answer that shows his threatening is getting neither good nor bad results.

[14b] You chose **negatively reinforced.**

No, because nothing unpleasant happened as a result of it. He was just ignored. Go back to the question on page 84, and choose an answer than shows there was no reinforcement of any kind.

[14c] You chose **extinguished.**

RIGHT! Nothing was happening as a result of his threatening so there was no point in trying it again. The repeated absence of any kind of reinforcement from any source will extinguish the behavior. Now turn to the next page.

YES, THEY CAN HAPPEN ALL AT ONCE!

Let us see how things could work if you applied all three principles (positive reinforcement, negative reinforcement, and extinction) to Whining Wendy. For obvious reasons, you will see that we are simplifying the behavior in order to identify the principles, so this should in no way be taken as a never-fail recipe.

Wendy has learned to whine to get her way. Obviously this has worked (has been positively reinforced by someone in her past), or she would not continue to whine. Understanding this is important. It keeps you from expecting an overnight miracle, or from hoping that just ignoring Wendy's whining will make it go away (be extinguished).

You wish to change Wendy's behavior so that she whines less, or stops whining entirely. Your number one problem is to decide what behavior you want to produce. Remember, negative reinforcement will only tell her what *not* to do. Too often we terminate our thinking at the *stop whining* point, without carrying it any further.

How do you want Wendy to get what she wants or needs? Do you want her to learn to say, "Please, may I . . . . ?" Do you want her to learn to flatter people to get her way? Do you want her to hit people instead of whining at them? Any one of these possibilities could become, to Wendy, "the other means" of getting her way.

As you think through the problem, you will probably conclude that the behavior you want to develop in Wendy is twofold:

[1] Learning socially acceptable ways of persuasion (politeness, making the other person feel good about himself and you);

[2] Learning socially acceptable ways of dealing with disappointment when she is not successful in getting what she wants (going along with the majority, being a good sport).

Now you will begin to notice the rewards of applying theory to practice. You cannot be vague in your thinking any longer. *Now you must identify the specific behavior you wish to change and then define with exactness the new behavior that your child is to learn.*

If you do not identify the exact behavior you want each child to learn, you will have no idea what it is that needs to be positively reinforced. Further, you must focus on the child's total behavior so that you avoid replacing one behavior with another that is equally undesirable.

We have now decided that Wendy's behavior problem is whining. That is what we wish to extinguish. We have also determined what kind of behavior we want Wendy to acquire. We set out to suppress the whining behavior in Wendy so she will have a chance to learn to say, "Please may I?" and be a good sport if her request cannot be granted.

We start by telling Wendy quite pleasantly about the specific behavior that we want changed. We want her to know what kind of behavior should be eliminated and what kind of behavior she should use in its place. That helps her to know what to do and what not to do.

Hopefully, most of the identification of what she should do comes from *her,* skillfully stimulated and guided by us. "What did you do when you wanted the doll? Did you get it? Can you think of a way that might have worked?"

It is very important to discuss with your child the behavior to be changed. This is essential for an efficient and economical use of time and energy. There is no point in trying to sneak up on a problem, or to hope that the child can *guess* whether it is the whining or her wanting something that is unacceptable behavior. That way only causes confusion.

Again, do be reminded that the words or the approach you use with one child may not be at all appropriate with another. The principles remain the same, however, whether or not the words change.

You can apply these principles to even very young children. All youngsters need to identify the behavior that brings on parental disapproval and the kind of behavior that is more desirable.

TIMES FOR HEAVIER-FOOTEDNESS

If the undesirable behavior of your child is of long standing, you may have to do more than merely extinguish it. It may be necessary to suppress it by negative reinforcement so another behavior can be learned in its place. Suppose you say, "If you whine, you will have to leave us and go to your room." Then you must watch closely, since the minute the desired behavior occurs it must be positively reinforced. "Good for you, Wendy, you're asking in such a nice way. Of course you may do it." This affirmative answer, of course, assumes that it is safe and appropriate for Wendy to do whatever she is asking. If her request is not reasonable, we praise or reward her for asking so politely and explain why we cannot accede to it.

As soon as the behavior that we want in Wendy (asking without whining) has been positively reinforced ("Good for you!") enough times so that it is more likely to occur than her previous whining behavior, we can remove the negative reinforcer that was there to suppress the long-standing behavior. In this case, we will no longer need to send Wendy to her room for whining because she does it infrequently. When we reach that point, we can extinguish the undesirable behavior that is left over by ignoring any requests she makes when whining.

At the same time, we continue reinforcement of the desired behavior by fulfilling her request if she asks appropriately. ("You have asked so nicely, Wendy, yes, of course you may go.") When you look at Wendy's behavior this is what you should see happening: As soon as she has learned *sometimes* to say "Please" and *sometimes* to be a good sport, we stop sending her to her room for whining. Whenever she says

89

"Please," we positively reinforce her behavior. If her request is reasonable, we accede to her wishes. Remember, if her request is not reasonable, we praise or reward her for asking politely and explain why we cannot let her do it—or have it.

When she whines, we ignore her and insist that others do the same. Hopefully the whining habit will disappear (be extinguished), while politeness in accepting your decision without fussing will occur more and more frequently as a result of the desirable behaviors that have been reinforced.

WHEN DO YOU DO WHAT?

You may not be quite sure when to use negative reinforcement and when to ignore (extinguish by no reinforcement). It will help if you estimate how often the undesirable behavior is occurring. *If it is a new behavior or it has not happened many times, try ignoring it.* If the child fails to get results (no reinforcement) he will probably abandon that behavior (extinction).

On the other hand, if the undesirable behavior has occurred many times, you can be sure that it has worked for the child (been positively reinforced), or the child would not still be using it. You can recognize that the undesirable behavior may need to be suppressed by negative reinforcement until some desirable behavior has a chance to become strong enough (as a result of positive reinforcement) to take the place of the undesirable one and be more likely to occur.

To accomplish this trade-off in behavior, we may need to use a little parental strategy on Whining Wendy. Extra positive reinforcement may come in praise such as, "Daddy, watch Wendy! She doesn't fuss when she doesn't get just what she wants. Look what a good sport she is." You will find, as parents have for ages, that few children can resist the strategy of a thinking parent. *Then* you have some good behavior to reinforce!

CHAPTER V

HOW OFTEN TO REINFORCE

You have now learned how to work with positive reinforcement, negative reinforcement, and the process that will extinguish behavior. At first glance that should make everything very simple.

Then why doesn't it always work? When you do everything exactly the way the book says, why aren't the results always perfect? After all, you conscientiously try to watch your child's behavior very carefully so that you will not positively reinforce the wrong things unintentionally. You are careful, when you suppress something with negative reinforcement, to substitute a better behavior. And you try to make sure that all of the things you do to extinguish behavior are appropriate.

If you have done all of these things day after day and yet see slow results, you or any other parent might begin to feel the buddings of discouragement. But don't despair! There are some other aspects to help determine why some things may not work as quickly as you wish them to. There are some answers about how long you must continue to reinforce each behavior before the result is finally achieved.

The fourth main idea in the theory of reinforcement concerns the **schedule** of the reinforcement. *Schedule refers to the relationship*

*between the number of times the behavior occurs and the number of
times it is reinforced.*

This means that, in your planning, you must compare how often
your child does something with how often you reinforce him for doing
it. You can say "Good for you!" (positive reinforcement) every time
Johnny does what you want. Or you can vary the schedule by saying
"Good for you!" every other time, every fifth time, or whenever you
happen to be in a good mood. What you do about your child's reinforcement schedule determines to a great extent the results that you will
achieve when applying the various kinds of reinforcement.

Decisions regarding the schedule by which you reinforce are usually made unconsciously. Unfortunately, these tend to depend on your
mood, how much the behavior irritates you, your general personality
factors, and your consistency in carrying out the schedule. It would be
better if this were not so. Decisions by you should be made very deliberately, at a conscious level. They have a direct bearing on the rate at
which the child learns a new behavior, and on the ease with which he
returns to an old undesirable behavior.

The matter of scheduling works like this: If you use a regular schedule of reinforcement (reinforcing behavior every time it occurs) you produce fast *initial* learning in your child. If you say "Good for you!" every time your child does the right thing, you will produce in him a new behavior quite speedily—all other things being equal, of course. But then you face the problem of sustaining the new behavior. Your child's forgetting speed is apt to match his learning—so when you stop reinforcing him, his desirable behavior may be extinguished just as rapidly as it was learned.

At this point you must be very careful not to give in to the temptation to throw up your hands and say, "What's the use?" convinced that all your efforts have been for naught. By changing the reinforcement schedule you can make your child's new behavior resistant to forgetting.

If you have been reinforcing the behavior that you wish to see retained every time it occurs your child will learn rapidly. After a time you need to change to an intermittent schedule of reinforcement. Then you do not reinforce the good behavior every time it occurs, but only reinforce it periodically. For example, you might reinforce the first, third, sixth, and tenth times in a series of ten responses. This intermittent schedule of reinforcement makes behavior more persistent and more resistant to being forgotten.

Let us go back to your child's table manners. For a week, now, your child has been washed and has been eating his food like a human being. You have reinforced him positively and he now looks at you expectantly for praise at each meal.

You decide he no longer needs to learn the behavior, for this has been accomplished. But you know that it is possible for him to forget a good behavior as speedily as he has learned it, so you have another task to accomplish. Now your concern is over how long your child will remember the new behavior (when he is at someone else's house and you are not around to praise him), or how long he will continue the new behavior if you discontinue your reinforcement.

To be certain that the child continues this behavior, you start an intermittent schedule of reinforcement. When your child comes to the table clean and eats politely, you give him a hearty reinforcer by saying, "David, you just never forget to be grown up." The next meal when he acts appropriately and looks to you for approval, you will appear to be busy eating your own dinner or talking, even though you are watching David carefully. If he follows a characteristic pattern, he will look disappointed but will settle down.

At the next meal, to eliminate any possibility that he may return to his old behavior, you will be watching him conspicuously and you will reward him by saying, "You just don't need me to remind you at all. Why, even when I'm busy with something else, you know what to do!" That ought to hold him without additional reinforcement for another meal or two.

The next morning at breakfast, you again heartily reinforce him since you remember that a spontaneous recurrence of the old behavior may take place overnight. On the same day, you may not say anything at all at lunch. But you may terminate dinner with a comment like, "David, you've been perfect at meals all day today without my even looking at you."

Hopefully, before long you can forget you ever had to worry about David at mealtimes. An occasional reinforcer, perhaps once or twice a month, will maintain the strength of his behavior and keep him from forgetting the new behavior.

WHEN TO USE A REGULAR SCHEDULE VS. AN INTERMITTENT SCHEDULE

A routine nightmare in the child rearing ordeal is the attempt to have the child keep his room neat—with his things put away, and his clothes either hung up or in the dirty clothes hamper rather than in a wad under the bed. After looking at some children's rooms, one comes to suspect that youngsters simply cannot stand order and are really comfortable in a rat's nest. And this might be perfectly acceptable if you were not concerned with developing the good habits of order and cleanliness that are needed throughout life.

To begin with, you need to understand the difference between an adult's and a child's ability to organize and maintain order. Also it is equally necessary for the child to have an understanding why the home needs some semblance of order and tidiness to make it livable for other members of the family.

Decide what is a reasonable degree of order for your child's age. Remember, you must be careful not to make the mistake of expecting him to keep his room the way a competent adult would. Next, you need to plan with your child so you both can agree on an acceptable standard for his room. Finally, you need to discuss with your child ways that will help him accomplish the task. Possibly you may need to help him at first. This helps make the goal achievable for the child.

Often it is a good idea to record the child's decisions on a chart or calendar using either key words or pictures. Then a record can be made of what gets accomplished and what does not. When your child checks off that his bed is made and his clothes are put away, the chart will remind him that the other items listed, such as his toys or books, also need attention. This chart system is also a good reminder for you. As you see the drifts of dirty clothes you are apt to overlook the made bed, the put away toys, and the hung up clothes! At this point you might erroneously assume nothing had been done—and do your child a damaging injustice.

With these things in mind, let us look at some possibilities for a regular or an intermittent schedule of reinforcement.

FiFTEEN

As you begin the routine of getting your child to do a better job on his room (he may be a toddler or a teenager) you need to reinforce his good behavior:

[a] **Every time**_____turn to page 98, top.

[b] **Every other time**_____turn to page 98, bottom.

[c] **At intermittent intervals**_____turn to page 99, top.

[15a] You chose **every time.**

YOU BET YOU SHOULD! A regular schedule of reinforcement makes for fast learning. Every time he straightens his room, you need to do something that will positively reinforce him. Now turn to page 100.

[15b] You chose **every other time.**

Not unless you are teaching only half of the time. You want him to learn rapidly. Go back to the question on page 97, and select an answer that will continually convince him he is on the right track and is doing a great job.

[15c] You chose **at intermittent intervals.**

After he has learned to keep his room in acceptable condition, this is a good idea. While he is learning, however, it will slow him down because the lack of positive reinforcement every time will make his cleaning less probable. Go back to the question on page 97, and choose an answer that will increase the probability of changing his behavior.

SiXTEEN

Once your youngster has learned to keep his room in acceptable order, you want to make sure he remembers it even when you are not there to remind him. To develop resistance to forgetting, you decide to:

[a] Continue a regular schedule of reinforcement
——————————————————————————turn to page 101, top.

[b] Change to an intermittent schedule of reinforcement
——————————————————————turn to page 101, bottom.

[c] Change to a schedule related to the degree of difficulty of the particular situation——————turn to page 102, top.

[16a] You chose **continue a regular schedule of reinforcement.**

That would be no change at all. You have been using a regular schedule and reinforcing him every time he has made the correct response so he will learn rapidly. Turn back to the question, page 100, and choose an answer that will make his new habit resistant to forgetting.

[16b] You chose **change to an intermittent schedule of reinforcement.**

RIGHT! Once a response has been learned and you sometimes receive a reward for it and sometimes not, you always have hope that the next time will be rewarded. Slot machines are built on the principle that if they pay off occasionally, people will keep putting money into them. The economy of Las Vegas proves that an intermittent reinforcement system works well. If people enjoy gambling, just an occasional pay-off will keep them playing. Once your youngster acquires the habit of room cleaning, an occasional pay-off from you will keep him doing it. Turn now to page 103.

[16c] You chose **change to a schedule related to the degree of difficulty of the particular situation.**

We would hope that your behavior would be relevant to the situation as it was described. However, go back to the question on page 100, reread the particular problem and, using what you have learned, choose the answer that will make keeping a neat room resistant to extinction (forgetting).

HOW FAST WILL IT HAPPEN?

No doubt you would like your child to achieve an immediate transformation from his less than perfect behavior to the kind of behavior you have always hoped for. Unfortunately this does not happen overnight. Like all growth, it is achieved slowly by degrees.

It will help if you think of yourself as a sculptor who is shaping your child's behavior. The sculptor does not take the block of clay or marble and produce a finished piece with only a few swift strokes. He begins by roughing out certain areas. Then he works with increasing precision to achieve the final result.

Like the sculptor, you also need to work with increasing precision as you help your child improve his behavior. First you must realize that you are not going to make a magical change in your child's behavior—from total chaos to instant order. As you begin, it is best to work on a few things at a time. Perhaps you will start his room cleaning by getting the clothes off the floor. To do that, you should reinforce the behavior that establishes the habit of picking up.

As another step, you might have your child bring the empty milk glasses and plates into the kitchen, so that you can reinforce that behavior. Next, you might concentrate on getting work and play materials properly put away, so that you can reinforce that behavior. If your child is old enough, you may wish to have the floor vacuumed and the furniture dusted, and you will reinforce that behavior until it becomes a habit.

However, the suggestions made in this book are only examples and should never be adopted unless they actually fit your family situation. The actual behaviors, and their order of importance at your house, are the ones you should decide upon.

How much you will insist upon from your child depends on many things: how much of the household routine he already knows to be his responsibility and how much he customarily leaves undone; how often he has temper tantrums; how difficult he finds it to play with other children without hitting, etc. A good rule to follow would be to *reinforce one behavior at a time until it is done without reminders.*

We know it is hard for a parent to accept just one improvement and be pleased with it when there is still so much to be accomplished. But remember, if you work like a sculptor and take care of one detail at a time as you are shaping your child's behavior, you will achieve the results you desire.

MORE ASPECTS OF SCHEDULING

Let us look at another example. Suppose you are trying to get your child to do his homework without reminders, nagging, or scenes.

You have already arranged in advance for him to set a time for his homework, before or after dinner. You have set the limits between which he can make his choice. When the time he has chosen arrives, arrange for him to be in a quiet place with distractions eliminated.

If you are watching a TV program, studying will be difficult for him so turn off the TV. This may mean scheduling homework times for him when one of your favorite programs is not being shown. Often you or your spouse can provide a model of concentration for your child that he will try to emulate. Try sitting quietly during the time you are seeking to develop the new study pattern. *You are his most important example and should try to do everything possible to help him achieve the desired behavior so you can reinforce it.*

If at first your child can concentrate for only a few minutes, you should accept that and reinforce what he has done. If you banish him to his room for forty minutes and he spends ten minutes for study and thirty minutes for daydreaming or restlessness, you have accomplished little. During a forty minute period that includes only ten minutes of concentration, your child may have practiced several bad habits that are destructive to study.

As he begins to increase his span of concentration and improves his study habits, his time for homework can be increased appropriately.

If you find it difficult to think of yourself as a sculptor shaping your child's behavior, try thinking about it as shaping up your body by reducing and firming up muscles. At first you lose a few pounds, then you increase the number of pounds that you lose. In the same way, you do a few push-ups, and then you increase the number of push-ups. While your goal may be a size twelve dress or the completion of fifty push-ups, you do not expect to achieve these goals all at once.

Remember that your child will not achieve the goals you set for him all at once either. But if you reinforce your child for each small achievement along the way, he too will shape up.

LET'S SUM IT ALL UP

You have now read four chapters, each describing one of the four important concepts in reinforcement theory. Let us review them:

1. A positive reinforcer strengthens the behavior it immediately follows.

2. A negative reinforcer

   [a] strengthens any behavior (desirable or not) that takes it away, and

   [b] suppresses the behavior that brought on the negative reinforcer.

3. Behavior is extinguished when it receives no reinforcement.

4. A regular schedule of reinforcement makes for fast learning. An intermittent schedule of reinforcement aids long remembering.

ON BEHALF OF PARENTS

These four main concepts are wonderful tools. With them, the one thing you can be sure about is that you can shape behavior as easily in your family as we can in a psychology laboratory.

It may not come easily at first. This does not mean that the tools are not correct or that they are not effective. It only means that by the time you read this book, your child has had a long history of miscellaneous reinforcement.

How many thousands of times has he interrupted, whined, fought, been sloppy, or been a poor sport before you were able to make a knowledgeable, effective effort to do something about it? Each unwanted behavior must have received reinforcement from you in one way or another, or your child would not be continuing it. *Any unreinforced behavior would have been extinguished.*

Not only has all this undesirable behavior been reinforced but you probably have unintentionally reinforced it on an intermittent schedule, which makes it even more resistant to extinction.

Over the years, you have probably attempted to change various undesirable behaviors from time to time but have given up. For example, you may have decided that you are no longer going to give in to whining, so you resist it a few times. Then one day you have company, or you are just too tired to withstand it, so you give your child what he wants.

This means that the undesirable behavior receives reinforcement from time to time. And this means on an intermittent schedule. As a result this unwanted behavior will be remembered, and remembered.

Before you read this book you may have been like the mother who said to a four-year-old, "I said No! And when I say No I mean it." The child was heard to reply, "You already changed to Yes once!"

DOING THE RIGHT THING

You have for many years heard yourselves admonished to be reasonable and consistent. We hope that you now have a better understanding of what it means to be reasonable and consistent, and of the reason for being reasonable and consistent. The inconsistent parent does not produce fast initial learning in his child because inconsistency means operating on an intermittent schedule. And the inconsistent parent does make the child's already learned undesirable behavior harder and harder to change.

As a result, the child has a difficult time changing bad habits he may have acquired, and he has an equally difficult time learning better habits of behavior.

You must also guard against assuming that the same thing that reinforces you positively will also reinforce your child positively. Whether or not you approve of what your child likes it is still true that what he likes or needs is what will positively reinforce his behavior and cause it to occur again.

You probably associate praise and reward with positive reinforcement, and punishment with negative reinforcement. But this is not necessarily so for every child. Think about a shy youngster. Can you see how he might find public praise very embarrassing and undesirable, and therefore a negative reinforcer? Now think about an attention-seeking youngster. He might find a public scolding very rewarding to his need for attention, so the scolding would actually be positive reinforcement.

It is always necessary to understand exactly what constitutes reward and punishment for your particular child.

You will discover what is reinforcing to your child by watching him whenever he is free to do what he likes. You then could use the activity, attitude, or response that you have observed as a reinforcer for him. If he likes to play outdoors, watch television, be read to, or talk to you, use these as positive reinforcers for the behavior that you wish established. Psychologically, we call this *identifying the reward system to which the child responds.*

AVOIDING THE WRONG THING

Unfortunately, punishing a youngster becomes so routine for many parents that it is very important to remind you again that *punishment is a dangerous weapon.*

It is true that you can suppress certain behavior rapidly with punishment but at the same time you may also develop other undesirable behavior. And if it takes away the punishment, you may unintentionally reinforce the bad behavior even further (lying, cheating, whining, crying).

Also, when you punish you cannot control the kinds of accompanying emotions and attitudes that your child may develop. Many destructive by-products (negative side effects) may be created solely because you have not handled punishment carefully (deception, deceit, insincerity).

Luckily, we do not need to worry about the effect of positive reinforcement and reward, since good and healthy feelings will usually accompany them.

But we cannot stress too heavily how much you DO need to be concerned about the negative feelings that may become associated with punishment. These feelings could become more of a problem than the actions you originally tried to change by using punishment.

Think about it from the child's viewpoint. Spanking and scolding Wendy may momentarily suppress her whining, but it may also cause her to learn that parents are mean, growing up is not fun, and that home is a place to be avoided by running away, staying out late, or by marrying the first boy that comes along. Knowing the dangers of using punishment as a management technique should be enough to make you want to rely more on positive reinforcers. The rewards of praise will lead to comfortable and healthy permanent changes in behavior.

Your understanding of reinforcement theory is critical to your success in working with your child. Let us apply your knowledge to the situation that follows and see how you do. Read the question and select your answer in the usual way.

SEVENTEEN

Now that you have a better understanding of reinforcement theory, you will realize that physical punishment (negative reinforcement) is usually not a good idea because:

[a] It is old-fashioned_____ turn to page 110, top.

[b] It is ineffective_____ turn to page 110, bottom.

[c] It is too hard on the parent_____ turn to page 111, top.

[d] It can cause undesirable emotions and attitudes
_____ turn to page 111, bottom.

[17a] You chose **it is old-fashioned.**

It is, but so are honesty and integrity. Being old-fashioned is not necessarily something to be discarded. Go back to the question on page 109, and choose an answer that describes why physical punishment is usually not a good idea.

[17b] You chose **it is ineffective.**

Often it is, although a good spanking may stop a behavior we do not like. There are better ways to change behavior however, so go back to the question, page 109, and choose an answer that will more precisely describe the undesirable results of physical punishment.

[17c] You chose **it is too hard on the parent.**

If you know anything harder than being a good parent, let us know. Granted, when you spank a child, it is an extremely unpleasant experience. But if it works, it might be worth it. However, go back to the question, page 109, and choose an answer that will justify your wisdom in using other means of control.

[17d] You chose **it can cause undesirable emotions and attitudes.**

IT CERTAINLY CAN! A child may learn not to do a certain thing as a result of a spanking. He also can learn to dislike you, that parents are mean, and that rules are not fair. All of these compounding factors make corporal punishment a negative reinforcer that usually is psychologically unwise. There are many other negative reinforcers that can be more effective and do not have such undesirable side effects. Now read on.

WHAT WE HOPE YOU HAVE LEARNED

As you have learned about the four principles of reinforcement we have tried simultaneously to apply these principles to *you*.

We have negatively reinforced you by sounding forth with threats of what is apt to happen if you overuse punishment. Clearly, we want to suppress your temptation to punish, so that you will always think about it carefully. Also, we hope to suppress any tendencies you may have to notice only the things that are wrong with your child.

We have suggested alternate patterns of behavior for you to use. We have talked about what they will do for your children if you do use them as positive reinforcement of your intention to use them. Remember that being *on again-off again* about using these principles will get you nowhere, so we hope the chances of your behaving in that manner will be extinguished.

Since, like all human beings, you probably are not as consistent in your behavior as you would like to be, you will sometimes forget to reinforce. So you will move from a regular to an intermittent schedule in applying these principles. Reading this book more than once will also reinforce your learning on an intermittent schedule and make your skill in changing your child's behavior more resistant to forgetting!
Good luck!

CHAPTER VI SETTING UP A PROGRAM FOR YOUR CHILD

Now you are ready to apply your knowledge of the principles of reinforcement to improving your own child's behavior. Isn't that why you read this book?

Let's review the main ideas and see how you can apply them to your child. If you have questions as you go along, please go back to the appropriate section for a more detailed review.

WHAT ARE YOUR FAMILY WANTS?

We must begin by talking about YOU. Look at yourself as a parent and as a wife or husband. What are your goals for your family? Do you and your wife or husband feel the same way about the goals of your marriage and for your child, or do you have different beliefs about these matters? Do you each have certain responsibilities? Do you both know what they are and agree to them? Who usually takes the leadership in making decisions? Think of your own marriage and decide which one of you has the main responsibility for seeing that your children do what they are supposed to do.

WHO DOES WHAT?

Let us put it another way. All through this book we are talking about improving your child's behavior. Who will really do this job? Will you and your husband or wife work out these methods together? Or do you agree that only one of you should be mainly responsible for making these decisions? Who decides what is objectionable or desirable in your child's behavior? Who is the disciplinarian in the family? Are you both agreed that this is the proper person for the job? If there are grandparents or relatives living in your home or nearby, what will their part be in making decisions and carrying them through in the improvement of your child's behavior?

Before you can decide about the specifics of improving your child's behavior, you must make the decision about who is responsible and how this responsibility will be carried out.

Some families decide that mother and father will participate equally in this task. In other families, the father is the head of the household and the final authority in all matters regarding marriage and children. In

115

other families, father is the provider and mother is the child-raiser. *No pattern is right or wrong.* You need only to know which family you are.

Consistency in applying these reinforcement principles is crucial to success, especially if you plan to change persistent misbehavior. Different approaches or disagreement between you and your husband or wife are easily detected by a bright child and will lead him to the undesirable strategy of playing one of you against the other. And he will always win.

Some of the decisions you make may temporarily interfere with your comfort or your usual way of organizing home activities. Sometimes it is wise to give up a little bit now to receive later benefits and joys. Remember that these inconveniences are worth it as means to important ends. Taking the trouble to do it right will pay tremendous dividends.

The ideas in this book are tools with which you can build desirable behavior. You must learn how to use these tools if you wish to achieve the results you desire. Your reward for persistent and wise use will be an *improvement in your child's behavior.*

NOW FOR YOUR CHILD

Remember, you cannot control all of your child's behavior. But you can encourage desirable behavior while you discourage or eliminate behavior that you find unacceptable.

The next step in your application of the suggestions in this book must be an objective look at your child's present behavior.

Spend some time watching your child while he goes about his usual activities at home. You may find it necessary to set aside a few minutes during each day to observe him. Write down some of the specific things your child does—but remember to notice *the acceptable as well as the unacceptable behavior.*

116

Now start watching for the kind of reinforcers he responds to, both positive and negative. We suggest you write down the results of your observations on the pages provided in this book. There are four lists.

First, make a list of the behaviors you wish your child to continue or to develop. Next, list the positive reinforcers you will use to strengthen that desirable behavior. Third, make a list of the behaviors you would like to change in your child. And fourth, list the negative reinforcers you may need to hold down undesirable behavior while you are teaching acceptable behavior in its place.

Remember, the only way to secure this necessary information is by careful observation of your child. You and your spouse may work on this together, or one of you may take the responsibility for it.

All set?

LIST OF BEHAVIORS

List A. This is the list of things your child does that you approve of and wish him to continue. If you overlook desirable behaviors you will extinguish them, and you don't want that to happen.

You must be specific about the good things your child does. It is not enough to ask him to be *good* in a general sense, since this vague statement seldom has any real meaning to anyone and consequently will not produce the results that you desire.

No matter how difficult your child has been lately, you will find that he does many things that really please you. You probably have taken these things for granted and seldom noticed them. It will help you if you list them.

Write the behaviors to be encouraged or strengthened in List A.

LIST A

BEHAVIORS TO BE ENCOURAGED

1. _____

2. _____

3. _____

4. _____

5. _____

6. _____

7. _____

8. _____

LIST OF POSITIVE REINFORCERS

List B. Now think of the things that are positive reinforcers for your child. These will be the rewards you will use to strengthen your child's desirable behavior and reinforce changes from his undesirable behavior. Remember, if he is just learning to act better or beginning to do something desirable, you must positively reinforce him every time (regular schedule). If the desirable behavior occurs often, you will reinforce him once in a while (intermittent schedule).

Only *you* can know precisely which reinforcers are appropriate for your child. For some children, a positive reinforcer is a special privilege. For others, it is an extra snack or a little toy that has been wanted for some time. With still other children, a word of praise or direct physical affection, such as a hug or a pat, is the most rewarding. It is up to you, with the knowledge you have of your own child and of his interests, to determine what really *turns him on*—what motivates him to repeat the behavior you want continued. Whether it is watching his favorite program on television or getting to stay out longer to play or going to the ball game with Dad, make sure your positive reinforcers are things that HE desires. Praise and approval are positive reinforcers that will be available to him all through life, so be certain you use them often.

Usually it is best to use a variety of positive reinforcers. The same reward for the same behavior, unless this has been a special contract agreed upon with your child in advance, can become monotonous and should be avoided. Changing reinforcers has the pleasant element of surprise and keeps your child guessing. It also helps to prevent the "If I'm good at the store, will you get me candy?" type of negotiation.

In List B write down a list of positive reinforcers that will work with your child.

LIST B

POSITIVE REINFORCERS

1. _____

2. _____

3. _____

4. _____

5. _____

SOME WORDS ABOUT REINFORCERS

Do not use the reinforcer as a bribe, such as, "If you do this, I'll get you that." Bribing a youngster will only increase his bargaining or negotiating behavior—something you do not want.

We mentioned before that it is effective to make your positive reinforcer a surprise. Let it come as a result of desirable behavior when the last thought in your child's mind is the possibility of getting a reward. Try a variety of things. *Adapt your positive reinforcement techniques to your child's needs.*

Occasionally a parent asks, "Why should I reinforce my child for doing what he should?" The answer is simple. You want him to keep doing it and improve his behavior.

Children who are having behavior problems often have had too little positive reinforcement. Rather than focusing on their desirable behavior, too much emphasis has been placed on undesirable behavior. As a result, these children have become hostile and difficult to manage. Just by working on positive reinforcement you will see marked improvement in your child's behavior and attitude. Also the general emotional climate in your household will improve.

REINFORCING OTHERS

You might also think about these same first two lists in relation to your wife or husband.

Because we are adults, we often assume that compliments and approval are not needed. Nothing could be further from the truth.

Think of something your mate does that you like, and let him or her know that you like it. You will be amazed at what this will do to increase pleasure and satisfaction from your marriage.

LISTING BEHAVIORS TO CHANGE

List C. Now you're ready to continue with the task of changing your child's undesirable behavior. Make a list of things your child does that are not desirable.

You certainly do not need assistance in thinking of behaviors you would like to change. But some of the following concerns are typical and may serve as reminders to you.

Does your child pay attention when he is spoken to?

Does he do as he is told?

Does he do his homework without you reminding him?

Does he act respectfully to you or to other adults?

Does he come to dinner when he is called?

Is he quiet when you are talking on the phone?

Does he go to bed when he is supposed to?

Does he argue or fight more than he should?

Does he get dressed on time in the morning before school?

Does he clean his room and brush his teeth?

Does he get along with his younger brother or sister?

Does he help around the house?

On List C record your list of behaviors that you would like to see changed. Then decide which of these behaviors are the more objectionable and which are the less objectionable. Write M beside the more objectionable ones and L besides the less objectionable.

Now, as you look at the behaviors you have listed, try to estimate how much control you have over the situations in which these behaviors usually occur. Underline those behaviors over which you feel you have effective control, so that you can react to them quickly and confidently when they do occur. You usually have the most effective control over situations that occur in your own home, when your child is actually in your presence, and when you can act immediately after the undesirable behavior occurs. *These are the behaviors that you will be able to change most easily.*

For example, you have immediate control of Mike's behavior when he throws a temper tantrum right in front of you, even though he may also throw a tantrum at Grandma's when you are not there. You can control his study habits at home, though you cannot do so when he is at school. You have more control over how he plays at home than when he plays at the neighbor's. Therefore *throwing temper tantrums, not doing his homework properly,* and *hitting other children* might be the underlined behaviors to be changed.

LIST C

BEHAVIORS TO BE CHANGED

STOP	START

1. _____ . . . .

2. _____ . . . .

3. _____ . . . .

4. _____ . . . .

5. _____ . . . .

6. _____ . . . .

7. _____ . . . .

8. _____ . . . .

9. _____ . . . .

10. _____ . . . .

On the dotted line beside each behavior to be changed, write the behavior you would like to have replace it. Be sure it is specific, or you will not know what to reinforce. Your list might look like this:

1. *using bad language*   using "darn" instead of "damn"

2. *hitting his sister*   telling you when he is angry with her

3. *interrupting parents*   waiting until parent is finished talking

Remember, when you tell your child to *stop* doing something, he needs to know immediately what it is he is to *start* doing; you must identify the new behavior he is to practice.

LISTING NEGATIVE REINFORCERS

List D. The last list you need to make is a list of negative reinforcers. Hopefully, your use of positive reinforcers will eliminate the need for many disagreeable consequences. If your child has developed undesirable behavior of long standing, it may be necessary to negatively reinforce that behavior so it can be controlled while you are teaching him better behavior, and while you are strengthening that better behavior with positive reinforcement.

Write the negative reinforcers you might use on List D. Try to make them the natural consequence of the undesirable behavior rather than a random punishment that you might inflict. Being *grounded* if he does not come home when he should, helping you clean when he has made a mess, working to pay for something he has damaged or broken, and staying by himself when he is disagreeable to others are all normal consequences. *Spanking, hitting, slapping, and scolding are not!*

Remember that what works with one child in your family may not work with another. Try to list the things that each child does not want to have happen to him: being deprived of privileges, staying in his own yard, getting the *silent treatment,* being sent to his room.

We hope that you will give first consideration to extinguishing behavior by ignoring it, rather than suppressing behavior by negative reinforcement. But we recognize that certain behaviors can be very resistant, and you may have to use negative reinforcers. Negative reinforcement has a different meaning from punishment, however. Reread the section on page 40 if you are not sure of this difference.

Be certain you are specific on your list. If your child loves to go out and play with other children in the neighborhood, you might keep him in the house. Withdrawing the use of his bike or his car makes a great impact and is a reasonable consequence of an abuse of privileges.

Watch what he does, however, to take away the punishment—for that is the behavior that is being strengthened. Make sure you are not unintentionally encouraging deception and deceit.

As with positive reinforcement, vary your negative reinforcers, starting with the less severe, resorting to the more severe only if absolutely necessary.

LIST D

NEGATIVE REINFORCERS

1. _____

2. _____

3. _____

4. _____

5. _____

GOING INTO ACTION

Now all four lists are completed. You have a list of behaviors to be encouraged, a list of behaviors to be discouraged, a list of positive reinforcers, and a list of negative reinforcers.

From the list of behaviors to be changed, select a problem with an L beside it and a line under it. This means it is a less objectionable behavior that is under your control. Starting with this problem you are apt to be successful on your first try! Now focus all your energy in that direction. Remember, at first, one behavior at a time will be plenty.

After you choose the first behavior to be changed, it is helpful to discuss with your child both the undesirable behavior and the new, desired behavior. *The more you and your child work together, the faster the results.* You should determine whether you will do this on your own or with your spouse. You may wish to use the improvement chart to let both of you know how well it is working. See page 127.

After you have successfully changed the first behavior and are using intermittent reinforcement, begin on the second behavior that you wish to change. Eventually you will broaden and enlarge your total area of improvement.

We have suggested that you start with the less objectionable behavior first since it is better not to tackle the more difficult behavior without practice and success in changing behavior. You also will acquire experience to make you more comfortable when using these methods with the more difficult and more undesirable behavior.

SAMPLE IMPROVEMENT CHART

(Record each time behavior has occurred)
Start with one behavior at a time.

ROOM	Sun.	Mon.	Tues.	Wed.	Thurs.	Fri.	Sat.	Total for week
1. Making bed								
2. Hanging up clothes								
3. Putting dirty clothes in hamper								

MEALTIME								
1. Coming to the table when called								
2. Clean hands								
3. Not arguing during meals								
4. Brushing teeth after meals								

SUMMARY

By now you will be better equipped to change behavior than generations of parents before you. Be sure you begin by *positively reinforcing the desirable behavior* with reinforcers that show sincere approval but no phony comments or bribes. You will be amazed how good behavior will increase, and at the change it will make in your home.

Sometimes this good behavior will occur as a normal part of your child's daily routine. At other times, you may need to devise a scheme to make this new or good behavior occur. Then you will need to determine how you will positively reinforce it. An example of this might be, "Let's quickly pick up your clothes so we can go out! My, you're a fast worker!"

Remind yourself often about the behaviors you are trying to encourage and be alert when changes occur. For example, if your child is too noisy, remember that *the time for you to act with positive reinforcement is when he is playing quietly or is reducing his sound level.*

Sometimes a strong positive reinforcement of a new behavior that occasionally replaces an undesirable behavior is enough to reduce or eliminate that undesirable behavior. When this happens, then you have eliminated undesirable behavior without any negative reinforcement. An example of this might be letting your child cut his own piece of cake when he finishes everything on his plate, which eliminates your need to fuss at him to eat.

If the undesirable behavior persists, or if the behavior is so bothersome or dangerous (running into the street, playing with fire), *that you must do something immediately to suppress it, then you are forced to use negative reinforcers.* Remember, any behavior that removes your negative reinforcer will be strengthened, so be careful.

As he begins to increase his positive behaviors, develop strategies that will cause your child to use his new behaviors frequently, so that you can positively reinforce him as much and as often as possible. Soon the desirable behavior will become habitual, and an occasional reinforcer will maintain it.

As soon as your child has practiced his new behavior sufficiently for it to occur more often than his old behavior, remove any negative reinforcer you may have used. After that, merely try to ignore the old behavior if it should occur. Thus, you move your method of handling your child from negative reinforcement to extinction of the problem behavior.

As desirable behavior becomes increasingly habitual, *change to an intermittent schedule* of reinforcing the desirable behavior. Then make the intervals between reinforcement increasingly long, so that the new behavior becomes more and more resistant to forgetting.

Realize that every child occasionally slips back into his old habits. Do not be discouraged by this, because it is a natural part of growth; it will occur from time to time. These slipping back episodes can usually be extinguished if you simply ignore them according to the proper technique. However, if the child slips back too often you will have to reinstate your earlier procedure by negatively reinforcing the undesirable behavior and positively reinforcing the desirable behavior.

Do not neglect one important factor in your thinking, namely, *the reason that undesirable behavior starts in the first place*. Perhaps a child is afraid he cannot succeed, and his bullying is only a form of bravado that covers up his fright. Perhaps whining is the way another youngster expresses unhappiness with himself and his role in the family.

Changing behavior by reinforcement in no way removes the cause of that behavior.

However, whining, misbehavior, and other forms of distasteful action are all compounding factors to an already unhappy child. They help no situation—they only make it worse. An anxious boy and a rejected girl inevitably incur parent, teacher, and peer-group disapproval. Changing undesirable behavior may not completely solve your child's problem, but it does prevent your child from becoming even more unwanted and therefore unmanageable and from getting into deeper trouble. And this goes a long way toward helping him develop into a fine adult.

You will find that much truly objectionable behavior can be changed effectively and quickly with the application of the four principles of reinforcement we have discussed. The many little things that seem to build up during the day can be controlled and the result can be a more relaxed, enjoyable home with mutual compatibility between parent and child.

It is also true that we avert serious difficulties in later years by preventing small problems from becoming fixed or major problems. Often merely improving certain child behaviors increases the satisfaction of the home atmosphere and, in turn, this happier base can change even major problems to minor ones. The next step, then, is to reduce the minor problems to the normal ups and downs of family living.

Even if your child has severe behavior or emotional problems, these techniques may make the difference between enduring parenthood and enjoying life with your child.

Do not be afraid to use these ideas. Picture the authors standing behind you saying, "Good for you! You really know how to use reinforcement theory!"

The best positive reinforcement for you will come as you experience the reward of your child's learning and growth.

Let us know how it works.